Gazzotti
Vehlmann

alone

4 The Red
Cairns

9th CINEBOOK
The 9th Art Publisher

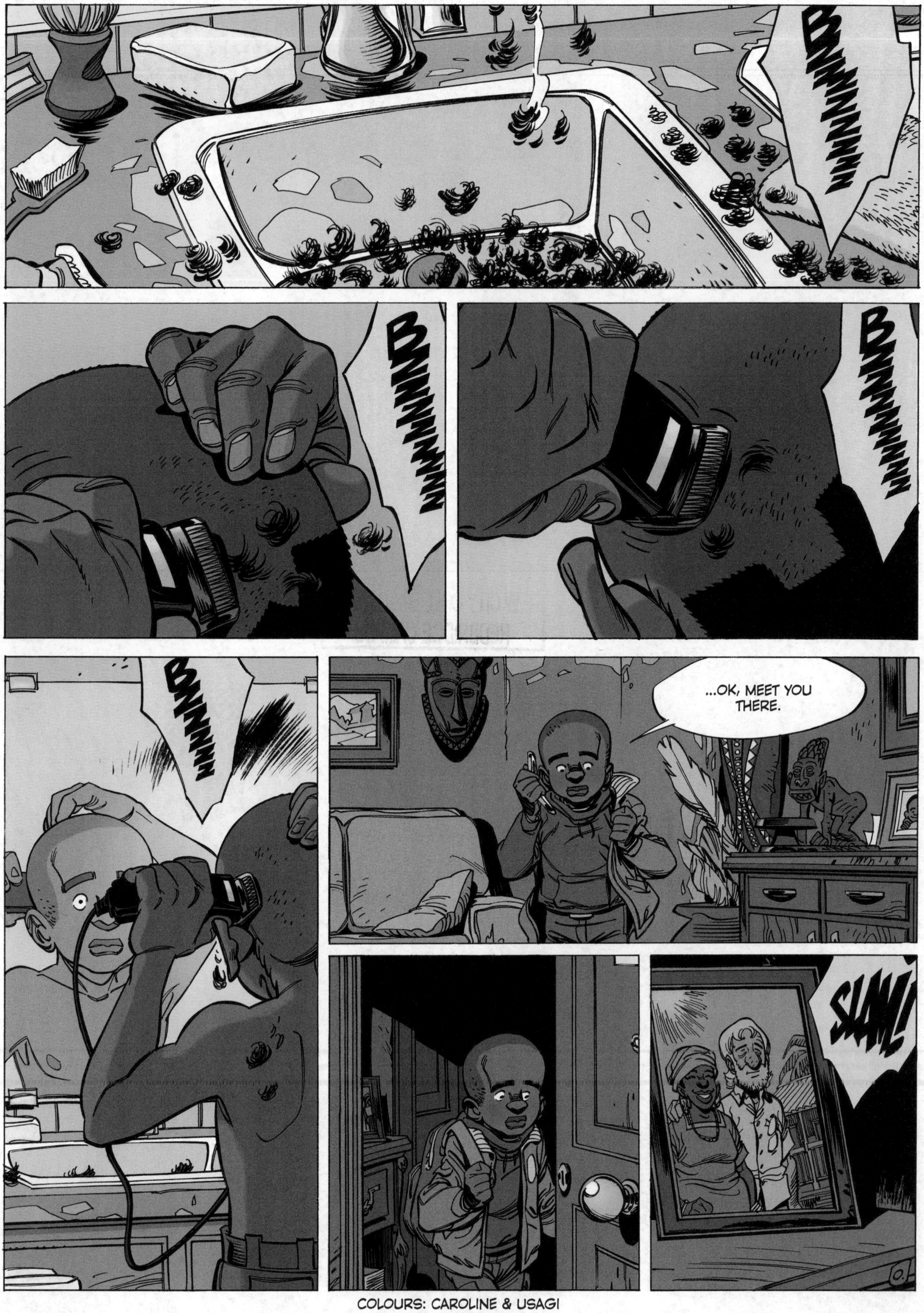
BZZZZZZZZZZ
BZZZZZZZZZ
BZZZZZZZZZ
BZZZZZ
...OK, MEET YOU THERE.
SLAM!

COLOURS: CAROLINE & USAGI

Original title: Seuls – Les Cairns Rouges
Original edition: © Dupuis, 2009 by Gazzotti & Vehlmann
www.dupuis.com – All rights reserved
English translation: © 2015 Cinebook Ltd – Translator: Jerome Saincantin
Lettering and text layout: Design Amorandi – Printed in Spain by EGEDSA

This edition first published in Great Britain in 2015 by Cinebook Ltd
56 Beech Avenue – Canterbury, Kent – CT4 7TA
www.cinebook.com
A CIP catalogue record for this book is available from the British Library
ISBN 978-1-84918-256-0

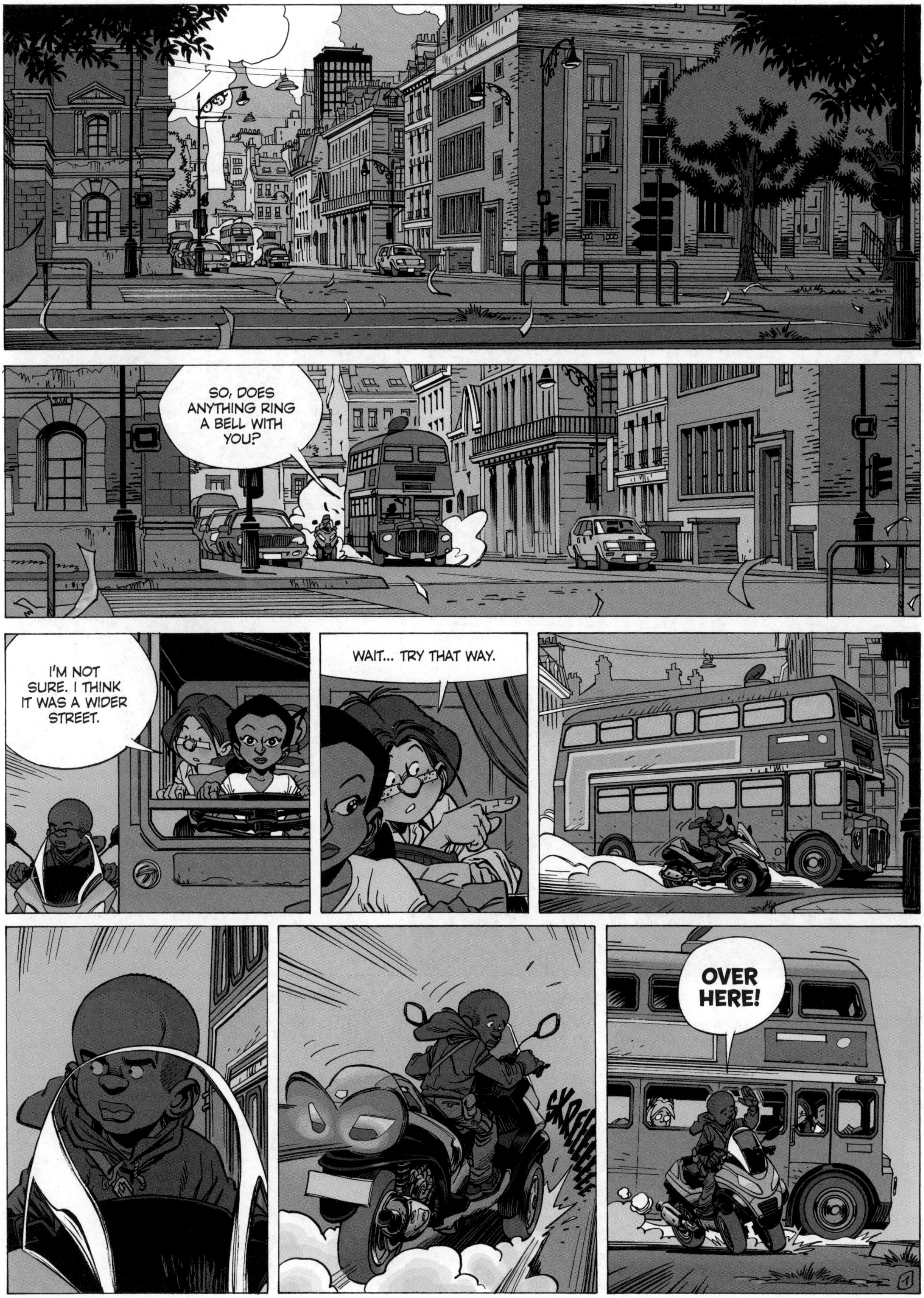
SO, DOES ANYTHING RING A BELL WITH YOU?
I'M NOT SURE. I THINK IT WAS A WIDER STREET.
WAIT... TRY THAT WAY.
OVER HERE!

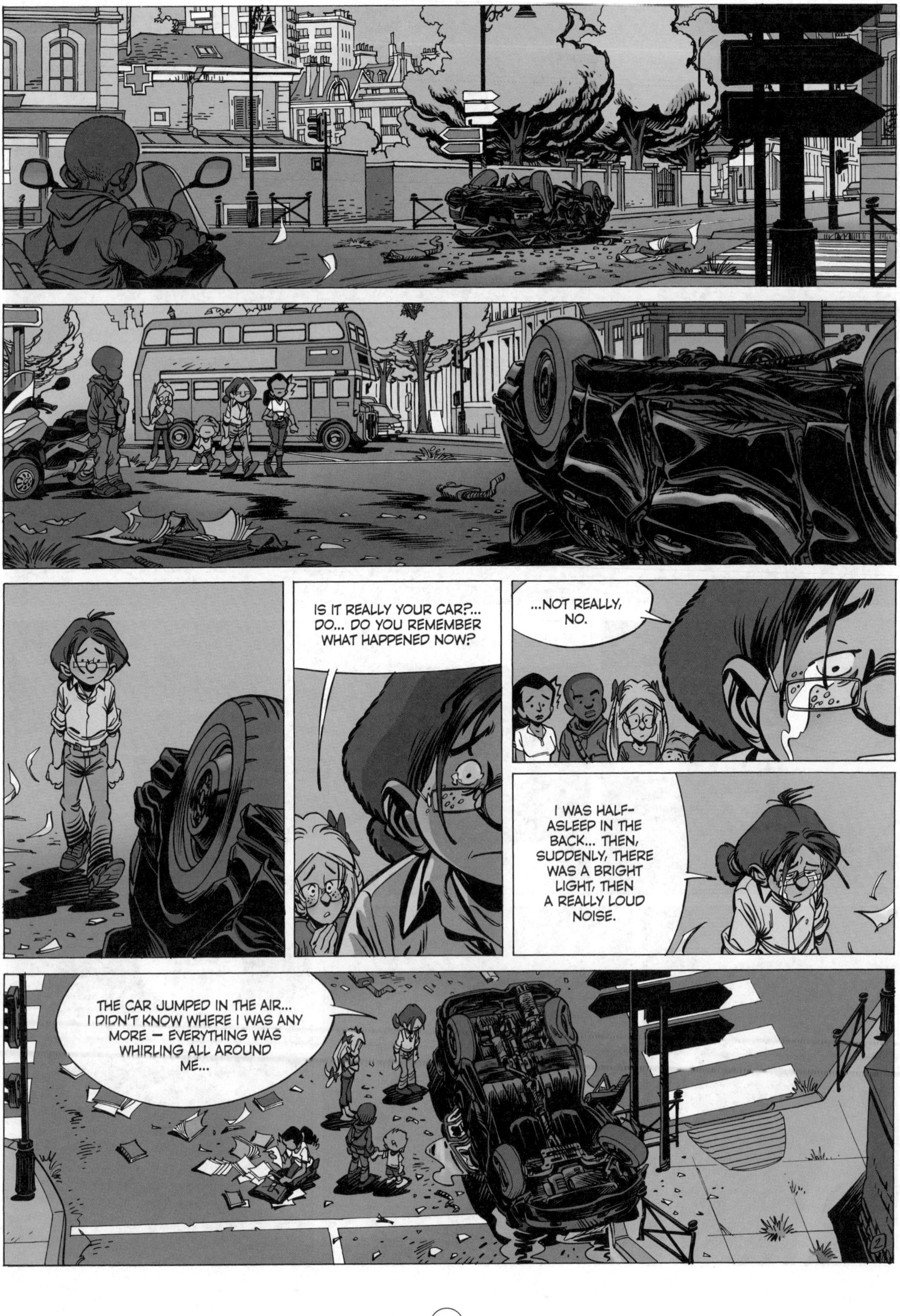
IS IT REALLY YOUR CAR?... DO... DO YOU REMEMBER WHAT HAPPENED NOW?
...NOT REALLY, NO.
I WAS HALF-ASLEEP IN THE BACK... THEN, SUDDENLY, THERE WAS A BRIGHT LIGHT, THEN A REALLY LOUD NOISE.
THE CAR JUMPED IN THE AIR... I DIDN'T KNOW WHERE I WAS ANY MORE — EVERYTHING WAS WHIRLING ALL AROUND ME...

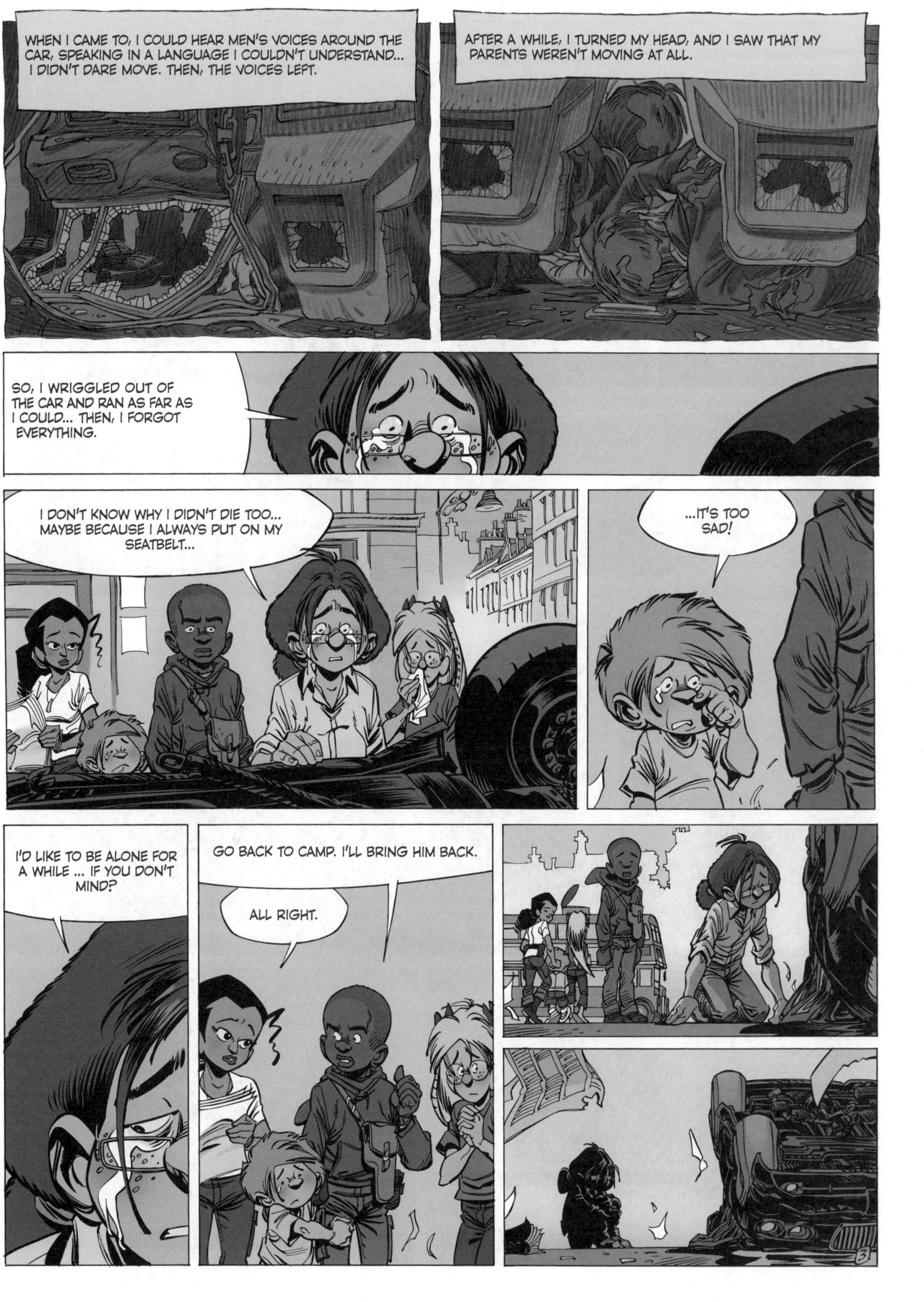

WHEN I CAME TO, I COULD HEAR MEN'S VOICES AROUND THE CAR, SPEAKING IN A LANGUAGE I COULDN'T UNDERSTAND... I DIDN'T DARE MOVE. THEN, THE VOICES LEFT.
AFTER A WHILE, I TURNED MY HEAD, AND I SAW THAT MY PARENTS WEREN'T MOVING AT ALL.
SO, I WRIGGLED OUT OF THE CAR AND RAN AS FAR AS I COULD... THEN, I FORGOT EVERYTHING.
I DON'T KNOW WHY I DIDN'T DIE TOO... MAYBE BECAUSE I ALWAYS PUT ON MY SEATBELT...
...IT'S TOO SAD!
I'D LIKE TO BE ALONE FOR A WHILE ... IF YOU DON'T MIND?
GO BACK TO CAMP. I'LL BRING HIM BACK.
ALL RIGHT.

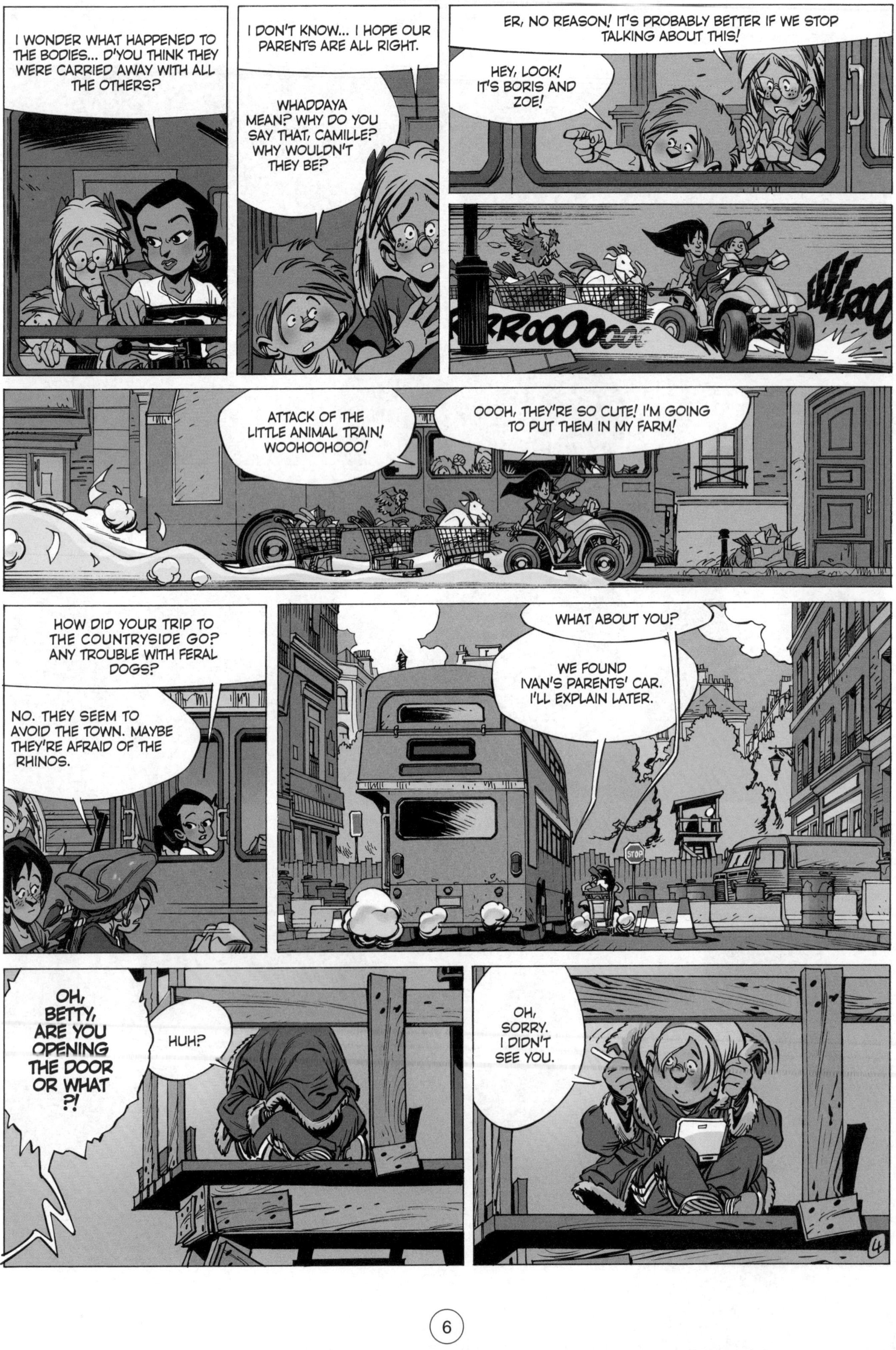
I WONDER WHAT HAPPENED TO THE BODIES... D'YOU THINK THEY WERE CARRIED AWAY WITH ALL THE OTHERS?
I DON'T KNOW... I HOPE OUR PARENTS ARE ALL RIGHT.
WHADDAYA MEAN? WHY DO YOU SAY THAT, CAMILLE? WHY WOULDN'T THEY BE?
ER, NO REASON! IT'S PROBABLY BETTER IF WE STOP TALKING ABOUT THIS!
HEY, LOOK! IT'S BORIS AND ZOE!
ATTACK OF THE LITTLE ANIMAL TRAIN! WOOHOOHOOO!
OOOH, THEY'RE SO CUTE! I'M GOING TO PUT THEM IN MY FARM!
HOW DID YOUR TRIP TO THE COUNTRYSIDE GO? ANY TROUBLE WITH FERAL DOGS?
NO. THEY SEEM TO AVOID THE TOWN. MAYBE THEY'RE AFRAID OF THE RHINOS.
WHAT ABOUT YOU?
WE FOUND IVAN'S PARENTS' CAR. I'LL EXPLAIN LATER.
STOP
OH, BETTY, ARE YOU OPENING THE DOOR OR WHAT ?!
HUH?
OH, SORRY. I DIDN'T SEE YOU.

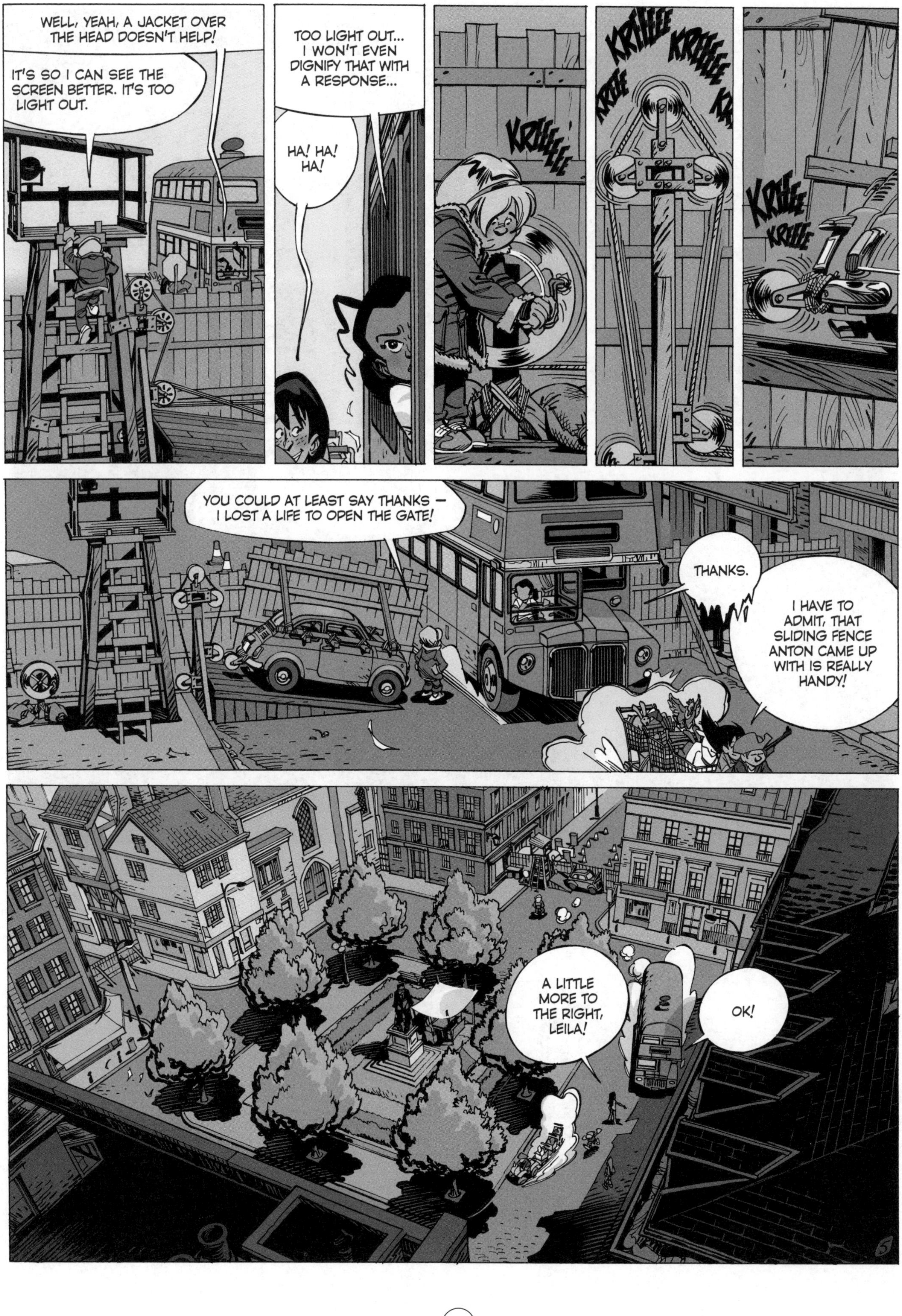
WELL, YEAH, A JACKET OVER THE HEAD DOESN'T HELP!
IT'S SO I CAN SEE THE SCREEN BETTER. IT'S TOO LIGHT OUT.
TOO LIGHT OUT... I WON'T EVEN DIGNIFY THAT WITH A RESPONSE...
HA! HA! HA!
KRIIEEEEE
KRIIEEE
KRIIEEEEE
KRIIEEE
KRIIEEE
KRIEEE
YOU COULD AT LEAST SAY THANKS — I LOST A LIFE TO OPEN THE GATE!
THANKS.
I HAVE TO ADMIT, THAT SLIDING FENCE ANTON CAME UP WITH IS REALLY HANDY!
A LITTLE MORE TO THE RIGHT, LEILA!
OK!

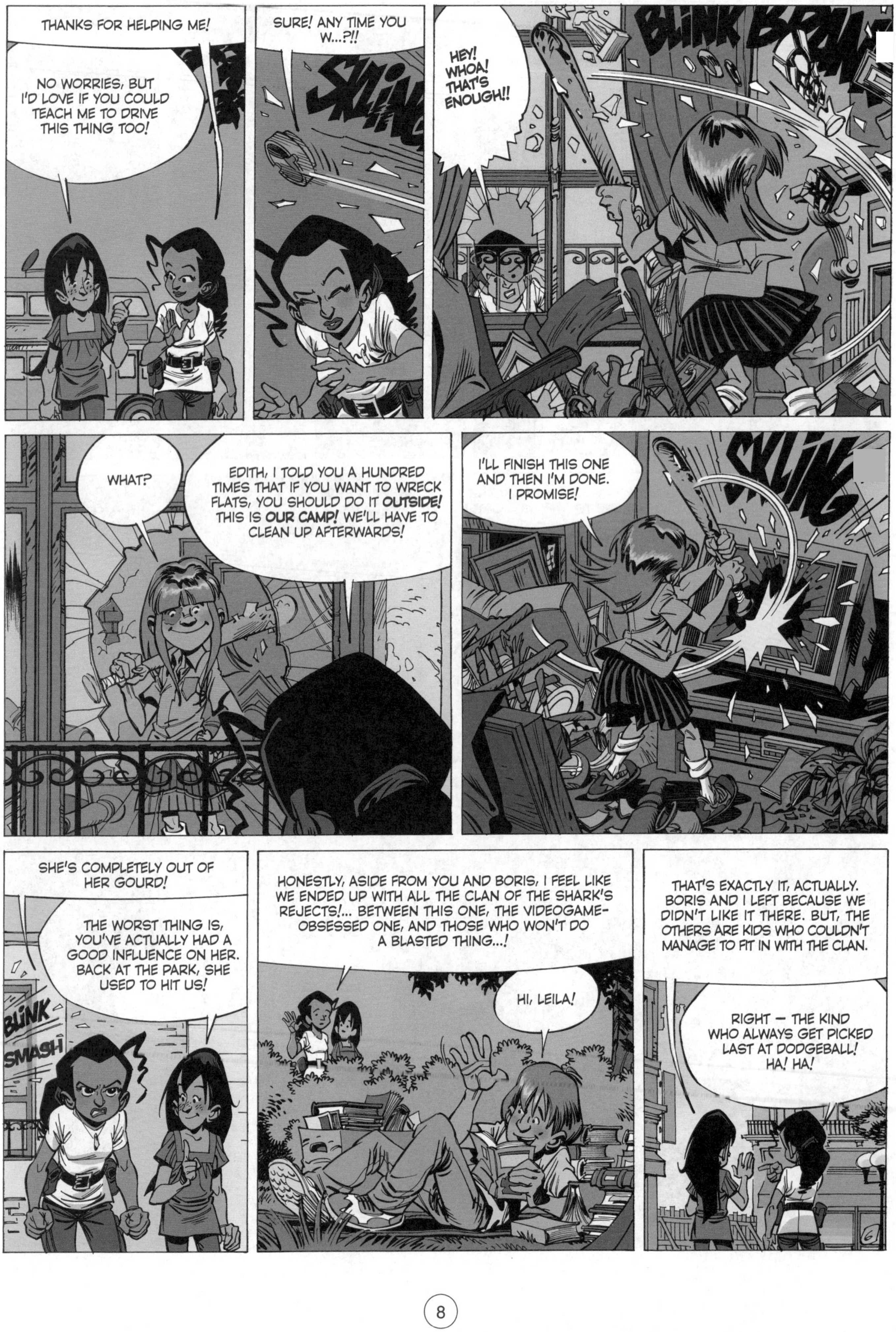
THANKS FOR HELPING ME!
NO WORRIES, BUT I'D LOVE IF YOU COULD TEACH ME TO DRIVE THIS THING TOO!
SURE! ANY TIME YOU W...?!!
SKLING
HEY! WHOA! THAT'S ENOUGH!!
BLINK BRANG
WHAT?
EDITH, I TOLD YOU A HUNDRED TIMES THAT IF YOU WANT TO WRECK FLATS, YOU SHOULD DO IT **OUTSIDE!** THIS IS **OUR CAMP!** WE'LL HAVE TO CLEAN UP AFTERWARDS!
I'LL FINISH THIS ONE AND THEN I'M DONE. I PROMISE!
SKLING
SHE'S COMPLETELY OUT OF HER GOURD!
THE WORST THING IS, YOU'VE ACTUALLY HAD A GOOD INFLUENCE ON HER. BACK AT THE PARK, SHE USED TO HIT US!
BLINK
SMASH
HONESTLY, ASIDE FROM YOU AND BORIS, I FEEL LIKE WE ENDED UP WITH ALL THE CLAN OF THE SHARK'S REJECTS!... BETWEEN THIS ONE, THE VIDEOGAME-OBSESSED ONE, AND THOSE WHO WON'T DO A BLASTED THING...!
HI, LEILA!
THAT'S EXACTLY IT, ACTUALLY. BORIS AND I LEFT BECAUSE WE DIDN'T LIKE IT THERE. BUT, THE OTHERS ARE KIDS WHO COULDN'T MANAGE TO FIT IN WITH THE CLAN.
RIGHT — THE KIND WHO ALWAYS GET PICKED LAST AT DODGEBALL! HA! HA!

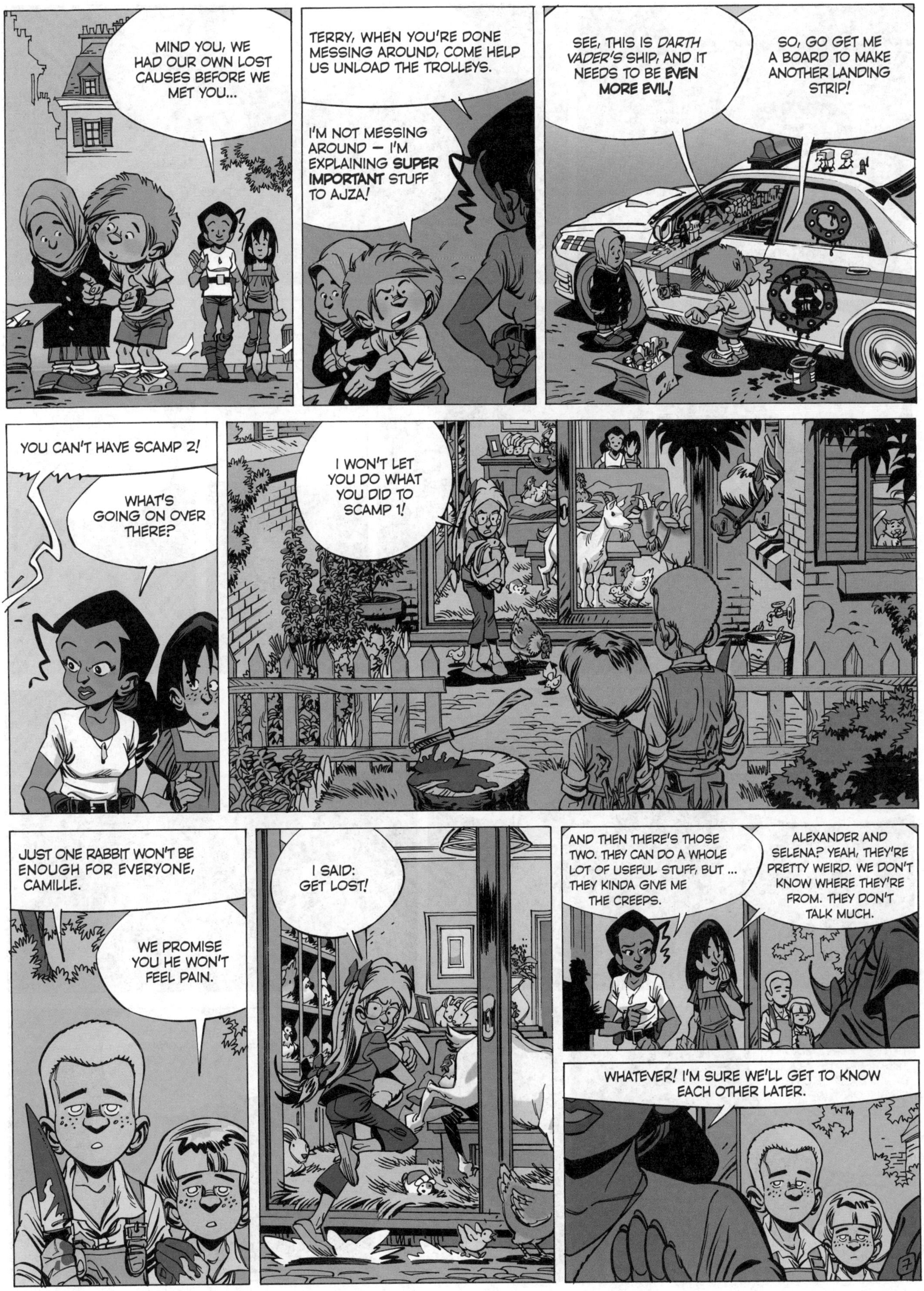
MIND YOU, WE HAD OUR OWN LOST CAUSES BEFORE WE MET YOU...
TERRY, WHEN YOU'RE DONE MESSING AROUND, COME HELP US UNLOAD THE TROLLEYS.
I'M NOT MESSING AROUND — I'M EXPLAINING **SUPER IMPORTANT** STUFF TO AJZA!
SEE, THIS IS *DARTH VADER'S* SHIP, AND IT NEEDS TO BE **EVEN MORE EVIL!**
SO, GO GET ME A BOARD TO MAKE ANOTHER LANDING STRIP!
YOU CAN'T HAVE SCAMP 2!
WHAT'S GOING ON OVER THERE?
I WON'T LET YOU DO WHAT YOU DID TO SCAMP 1!
JUST ONE RABBIT WON'T BE ENOUGH FOR EVERYONE, CAMILLE.
WE PROMISE YOU HE WON'T FEEL PAIN.
I SAID: GET LOST!
AND THEN THERE'S THOSE TWO. THEY CAN DO A WHOLE LOT OF USEFUL STUFF, BUT ... THEY KINDA GIVE ME THE CREEPS.
ALEXANDER AND SELENA? YEAH, THEY'RE PRETTY WEIRD. WE DON'T KNOW WHERE THEY'RE FROM. THEY DON'T TALK MUCH.
WHATEVER! I'M SURE WE'LL GET TO KNOW EACH OTHER LATER.

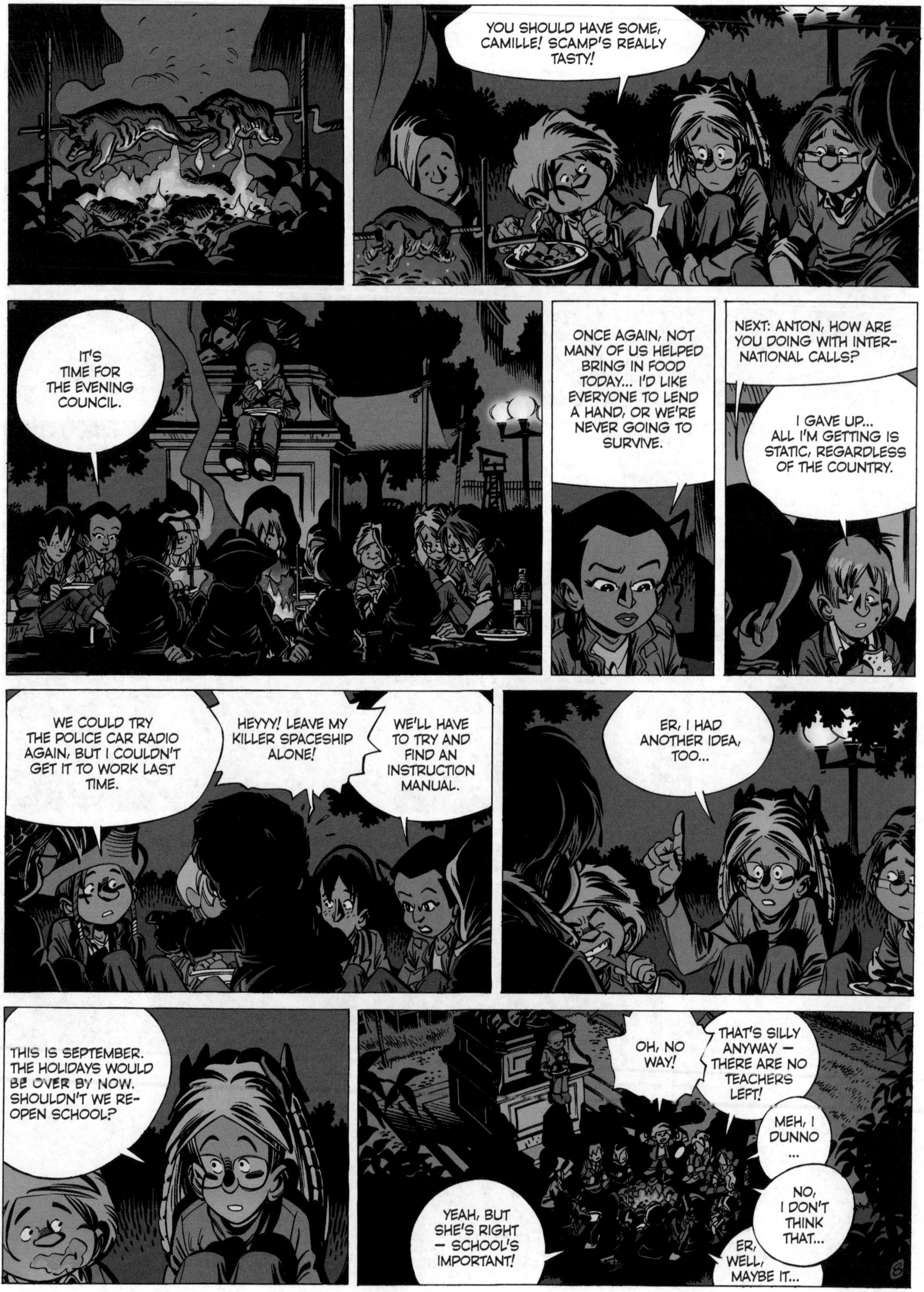
YOU SHOULD HAVE SOME, CAMILLE! SCAMP'S REALLY TASTY!
IT'S TIME FOR THE EVENING COUNCIL.
ONCE AGAIN, NOT MANY OF US HELPED BRING IN FOOD TODAY... I'D LIKE EVERYONE TO LEND A HAND, OR WE'RE NEVER GOING TO SURVIVE.
NEXT: ANTON, HOW ARE YOU DOING WITH INTERNATIONAL CALLS?
I GAVE UP... ALL I'M GETTING IS STATIC, REGARDLESS OF THE COUNTRY.
WE COULD TRY THE POLICE CAR RADIO AGAIN, BUT I COULDN'T GET IT TO WORK LAST TIME.
HEYYY! LEAVE MY KILLER SPACESHIP ALONE!
WE'LL HAVE TO TRY AND FIND AN INSTRUCTION MANUAL.
ER, I HAD ANOTHER IDEA, TOO...
THIS IS SEPTEMBER. THE HOLIDAYS WOULD BE OVER BY NOW. SHOULDN'T WE REOPEN SCHOOL?
OH, NO WAY!
THAT'S SILLY ANYWAY — THERE ARE NO TEACHERS LEFT!
MEH, I DUNNO ...
YEAH, BUT SHE'S RIGHT — SCHOOL'S IMPORTANT!
NO, I DON'T THINK THAT...
ER, WELL, MAYBE IT...

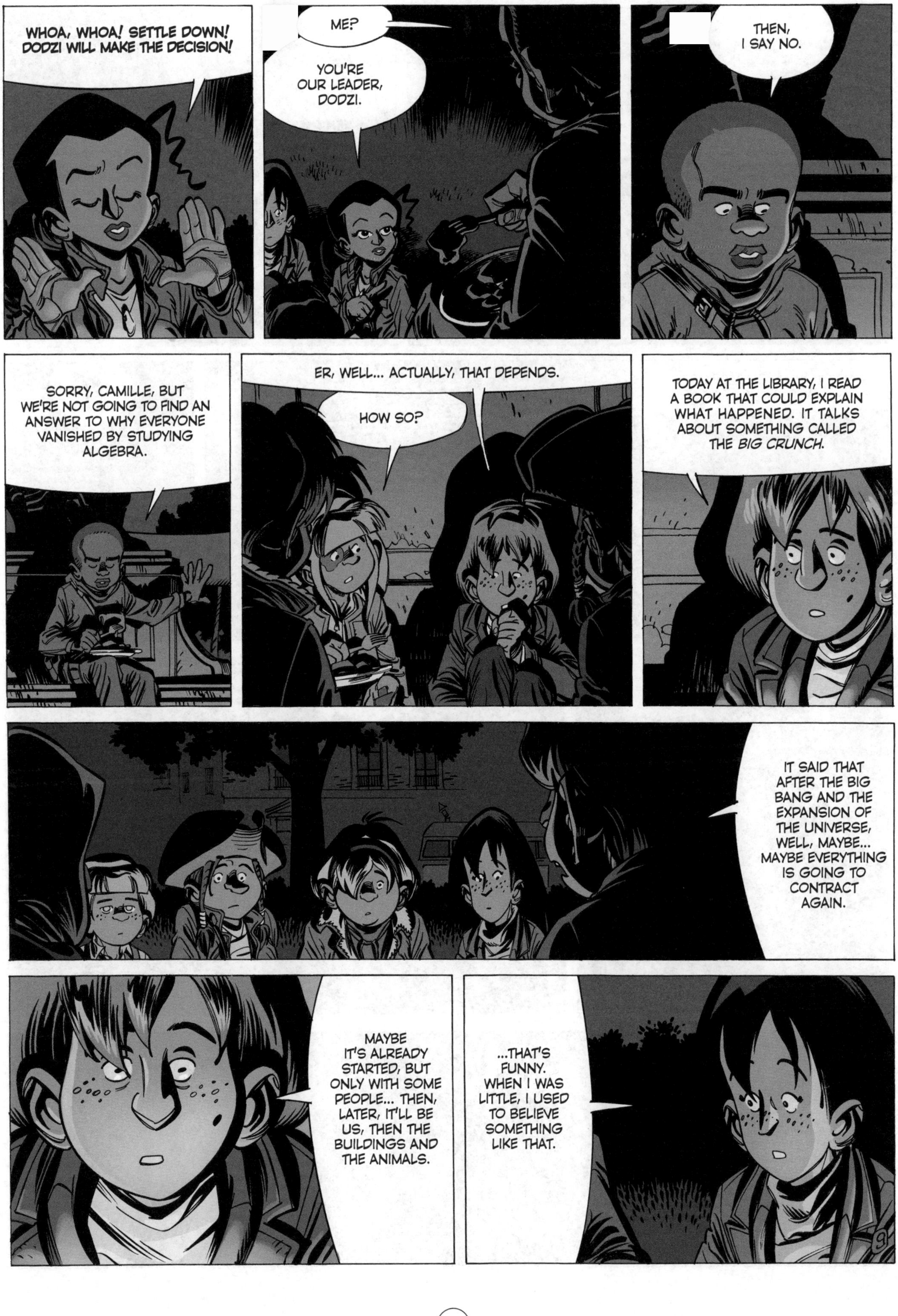
WHOA, WHOA! SETTLE DOWN! DODZI WILL MAKE THE DECISION!
ME?
YOU'RE OUR LEADER, DODZI.
THEN, I SAY NO.
SORRY, CAMILLE, BUT WE'RE NOT GOING TO FIND AN ANSWER TO WHY EVERYONE VANISHED BY STUDYING ALGEBRA.
ER, WELL... ACTUALLY, THAT DEPENDS.
HOW SO?
TODAY AT THE LIBRARY, I READ A BOOK THAT COULD EXPLAIN WHAT HAPPENED. IT TALKS ABOUT SOMETHING CALLED THE *BIG CRUNCH*.
IT SAID THAT AFTER THE BIG BANG AND THE EXPANSION OF THE UNIVERSE, WELL, MAYBE... MAYBE EVERYTHING IS GOING TO CONTRACT AGAIN.
MAYBE IT'S ALREADY STARTED, BUT ONLY WITH SOME PEOPLE... THEN, LATER, IT'LL BE US, THEN THE BUILDINGS AND THE ANIMALS.
...THAT'S FUNNY. WHEN I WAS LITTLE, I USED TO BELIEVE SOMETHING LIKE THAT.

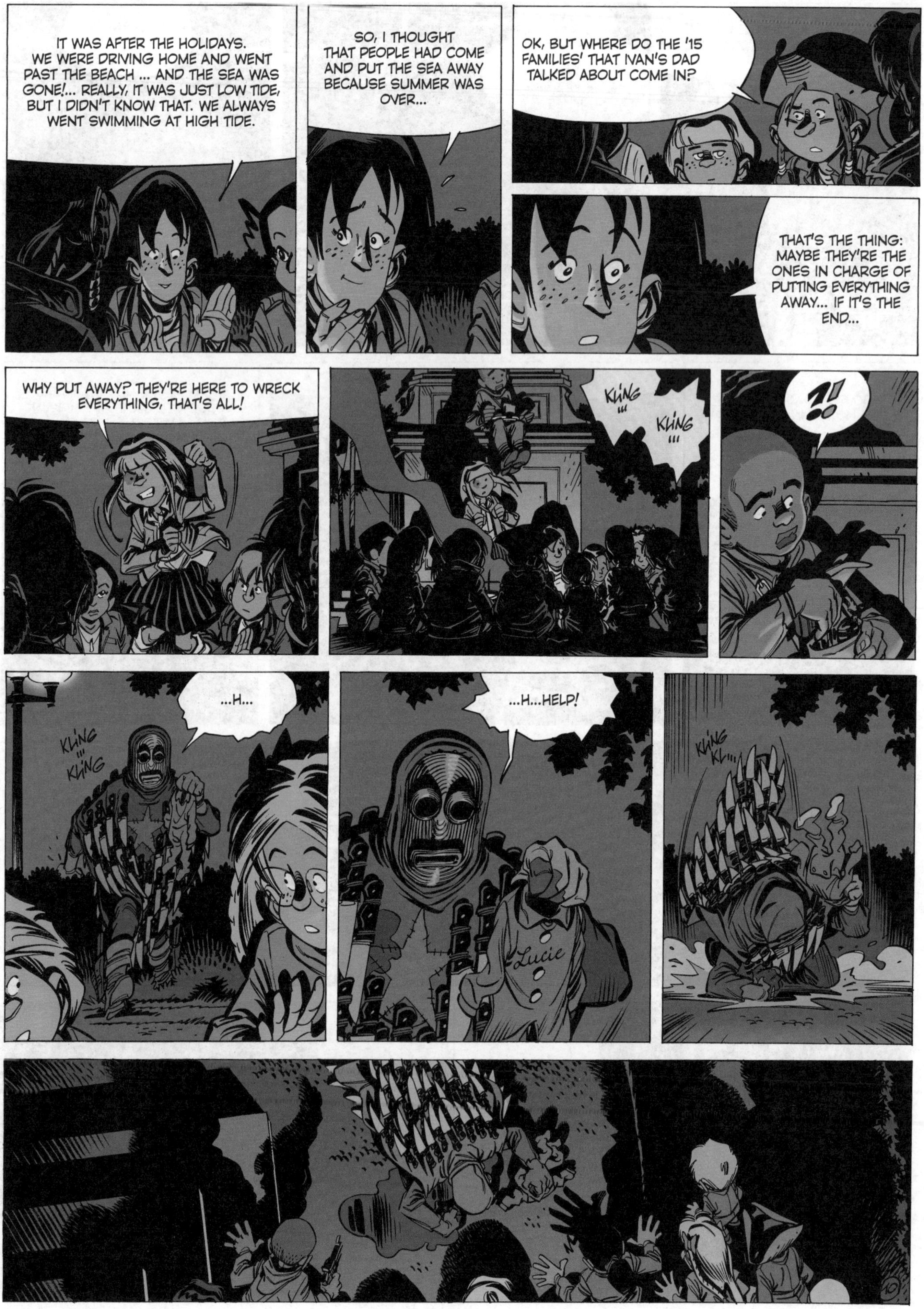
IT WAS AFTER THE HOLIDAYS. WE WERE DRIVING HOME AND WENT PAST THE BEACH ... AND THE SEA WAS GONE!... REALLY, IT WAS JUST LOW TIDE, BUT I DIDN'T KNOW THAT. WE ALWAYS WENT SWIMMING AT HIGH TIDE.
SO, I THOUGHT THAT PEOPLE HAD COME AND PUT THE SEA AWAY BECAUSE SUMMER WAS OVER...
OK, BUT WHERE DO THE '15 FAMILIES' THAT IVAN'S DAD TALKED ABOUT COME IN?
THAT'S THE THING: MAYBE THEY'RE THE ONES IN CHARGE OF PUTTING EVERYTHING AWAY... IF IT'S THE END...
WHY PUT AWAY? THEY'RE HERE TO WRECK EVERYTHING, THAT'S ALL!
KLING
KLING
?!
KLING KLING
...H...
...H...HELP!
Lucie
KLING KL...

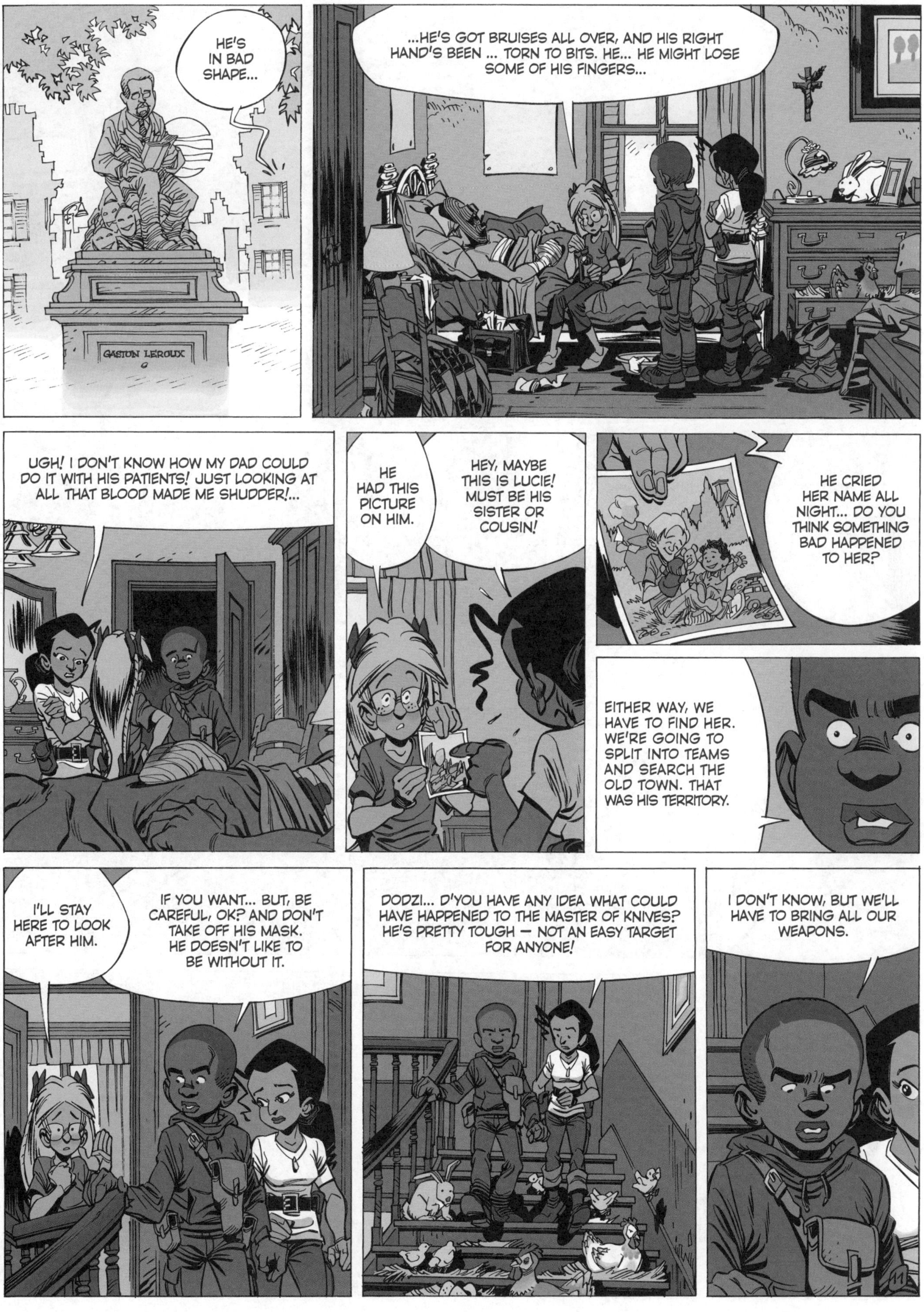
HE'S IN BAD SHAPE...
GASTON LEROUX
...HE'S GOT BRUISES ALL OVER, AND HIS RIGHT HAND'S BEEN ... TORN TO BITS. HE... HE MIGHT LOSE SOME OF HIS FINGERS...
UGH! I DON'T KNOW HOW MY DAD COULD DO IT WITH HIS PATIENTS! JUST LOOKING AT ALL THAT BLOOD MADE ME SHUDDER!...
HE HAD THIS PICTURE ON HIM.
HEY, MAYBE THIS IS LUCIE! MUST BE HIS SISTER OR COUSIN!
HE CRIED HER NAME ALL NIGHT... DO YOU THINK SOMETHING BAD HAPPENED TO HER?
EITHER WAY, WE HAVE TO FIND HER. WE'RE GOING TO SPLIT INTO TEAMS AND SEARCH THE OLD TOWN. THAT WAS HIS TERRITORY.
I'LL STAY HERE TO LOOK AFTER HIM.
IF YOU WANT... BUT, BE CAREFUL, OK? AND DON'T TAKE OFF HIS MASK. HE DOESN'T LIKE TO BE WITHOUT IT.
DODZI... D'YOU HAVE ANY IDEA WHAT COULD HAVE HAPPENED TO THE MASTER OF KNIVES? HE'S PRETTY TOUGH — NOT AN EASY TARGET FOR ANYONE!
I DON'T KNOW, BUT WE'LL HAVE TO BRING ALL OUR WEAPONS.

IVAN, GRAB A WEAPON. YOU'RE COMING WITH US.

...I'M NOT SURE I'LL BE MUCH HELP... I...

I'M THE BOSS. HURRY UP.

I'D RATHER YOU TWO STAYED HERE.

WHY?

SOMEONE NEEDS TO GUARD THE CAMP, JUST IN CASE ... AND I KNOW I CAN COUNT ON YOU.

YES, DODZI.

LET'S SPLIT INTO THREE GROUPS. BORIS, START FROM THE OTHER SIDE OF THE OLD TOWN. AND LET'S KEEP IN REGULAR CONTACT, OK?

OK.

KRÉÉÉÉÉÉ
KRÉÉÉÉÉÉ
KRÉÉÉÉÉÉ

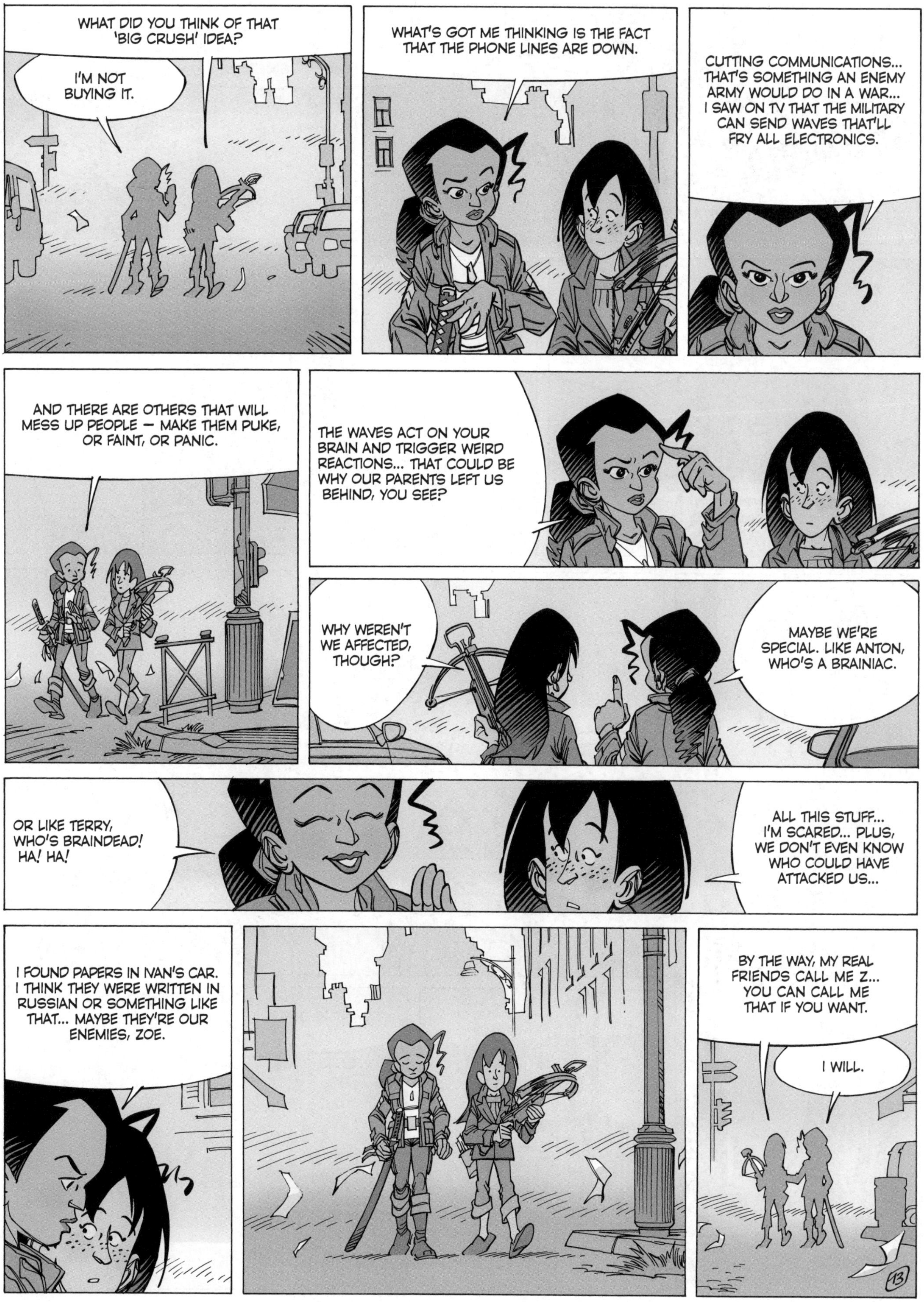
WHAT DID YOU THINK OF THAT 'BIG CRUSH' IDEA?
I'M NOT BUYING IT.
WHAT'S GOT ME THINKING IS THE FACT THAT THE PHONE LINES ARE DOWN.
CUTTING COMMUNICATIONS... THAT'S SOMETHING AN ENEMY ARMY WOULD DO IN A WAR... I SAW ON TV THAT THE MILITARY CAN SEND WAVES THAT'LL FRY ALL ELECTRONICS.
AND THERE ARE OTHERS THAT WILL MESS UP PEOPLE — MAKE THEM PUKE, OR FAINT, OR PANIC.
THE WAVES ACT ON YOUR BRAIN AND TRIGGER WEIRD REACTIONS... THAT COULD BE WHY OUR PARENTS LEFT US BEHIND, YOU SEE?
WHY WEREN'T WE AFFECTED, THOUGH?
MAYBE WE'RE SPECIAL. LIKE ANTON, WHO'S A BRAINIAC.
OR LIKE TERRY, WHO'S BRAINDEAD! HA! HA!
ALL THIS STUFF... I'M SCARED... PLUS, WE DON'T EVEN KNOW WHO COULD HAVE ATTACKED US...
I FOUND PAPERS IN IVAN'S CAR. I THINK THEY WERE WRITTEN IN RUSSIAN OR SOMETHING LIKE THAT... MAYBE THEY'RE OUR ENEMIES, ZOE.
BY THE WAY, MY REAL FRIENDS CALL ME Z... YOU CAN CALL ME THAT IF YOU WANT.
I WILL.
13

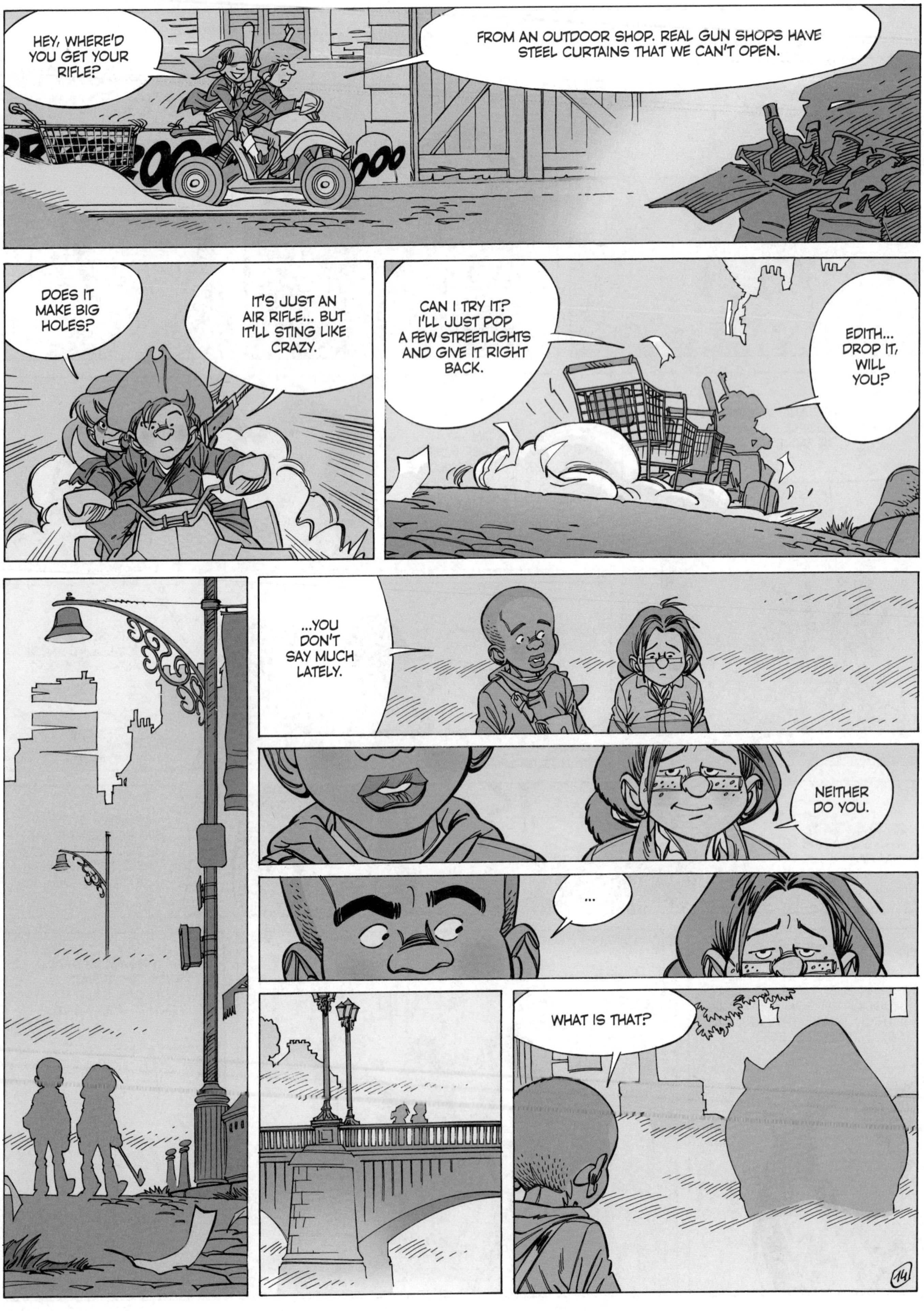
HEY, WHERE'D YOU GET YOUR RIFLE?
FROM AN OUTDOOR SHOP. REAL GUN SHOPS HAVE STEEL CURTAINS THAT WE CAN'T OPEN.
DOES IT MAKE BIG HOLES?
IT'S JUST AN AIR RIFLE... BUT IT'LL STING LIKE CRAZY.
CAN I TRY IT? I'LL JUST POP A FEW STREETLIGHTS AND GIVE IT RIGHT BACK.
EDITH... DROP IT, WILL YOU?
...YOU DON'T SAY MUCH LATELY.
NEITHER DO YOU.
...
WHAT IS THAT?
14

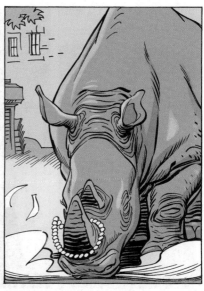

STAY AWAY, JEWEL...
DON'T MAKE ME HURT
YOU...

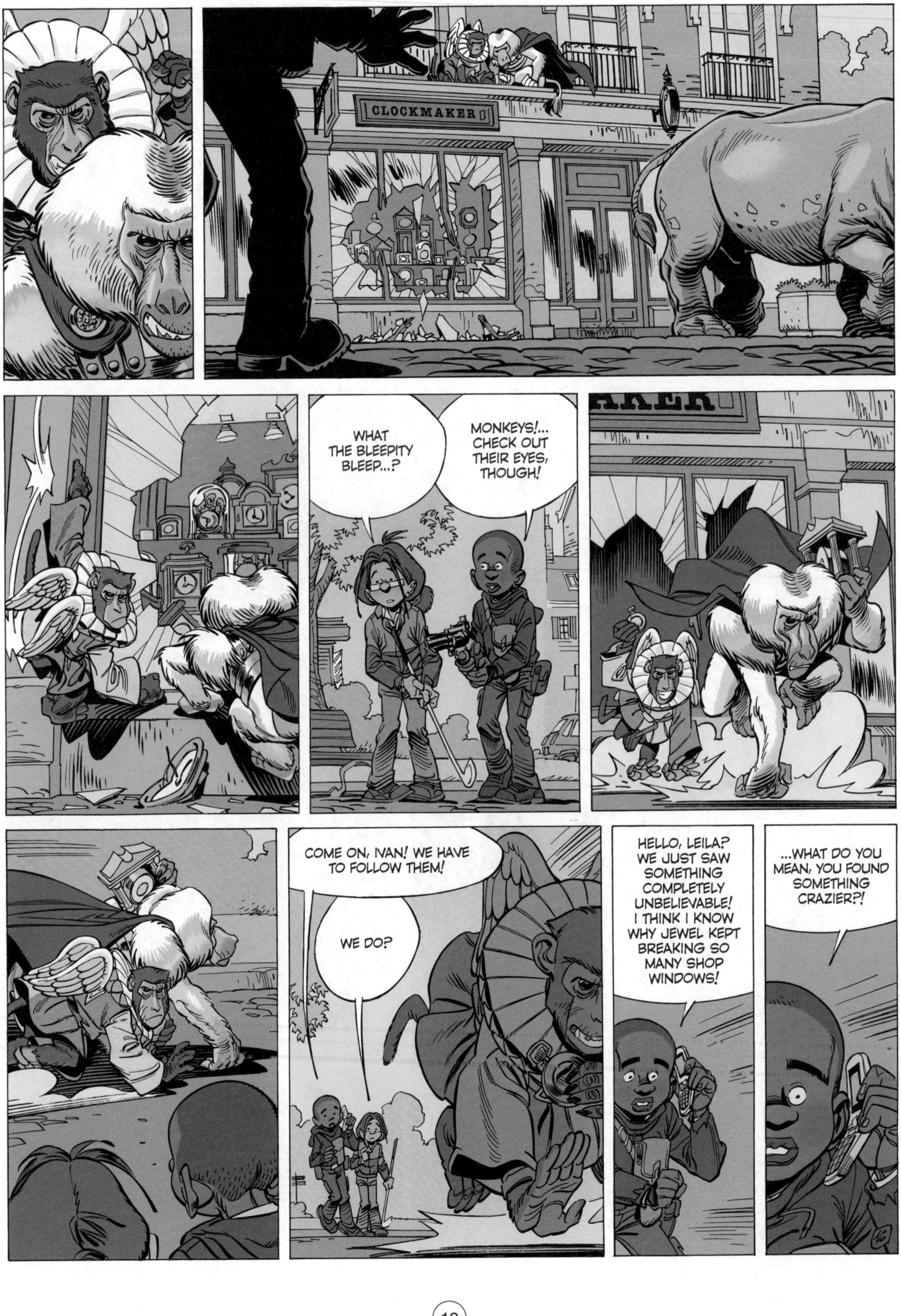
CLOCKMAKER
WHAT THE BLEEPITY BLEEP...?
MONKEYS!... CHECK OUT THEIR EYES, THOUGH!
COME ON, IVAN! WE HAVE TO FOLLOW THEM!
WE DO?
HELLO, LEILA? WE JUST SAW SOMETHING COMPLETELY UNBELIEVABLE! I THINK I KNOW WHY JEWEL KEPT BREAKING SO MANY SHOP WINDOWS!
...WHAT DO YOU MEAN, YOU FOUND SOMETHING CRAZIER?!

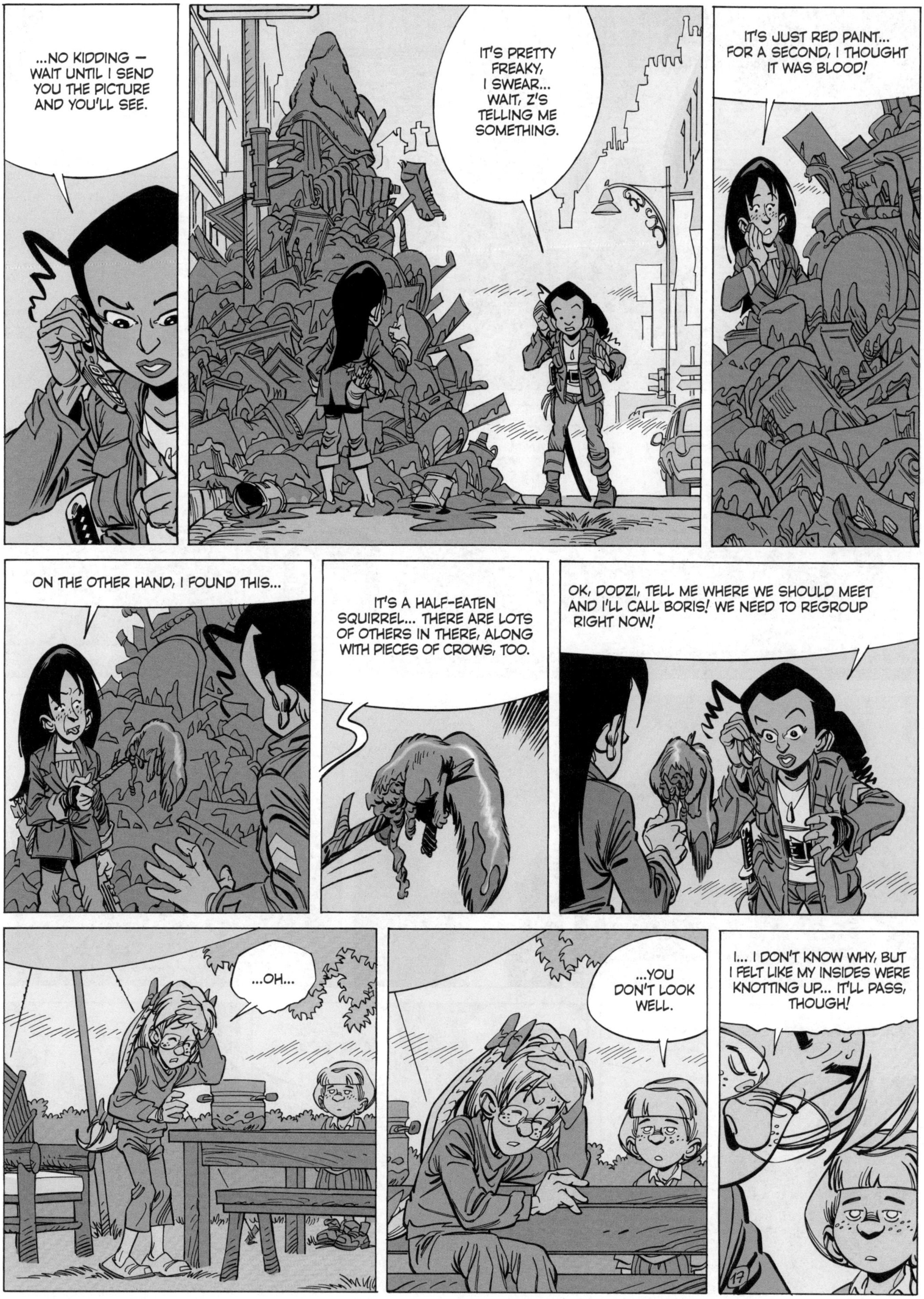

...NO KIDDING — WAIT UNTIL I SEND YOU THE PICTURE AND YOU'LL SEE.
IT'S PRETTY FREAKY, I SWEAR... WAIT, Z'S TELLING ME SOMETHING.
IT'S JUST RED PAINT... FOR A SECOND, I THOUGHT IT WAS BLOOD!
ON THE OTHER HAND, I FOUND THIS...
IT'S A HALF-EATEN SQUIRREL... THERE ARE LOTS OF OTHERS IN THERE, ALONG WITH PIECES OF CROWS, TOO.
OK, DODZI, TELL ME WHERE WE SHOULD MEET AND I'LL CALL BORIS! WE NEED TO REGROUP RIGHT NOW!
...OH...
...YOU DON'T LOOK WELL.
I... I DON'T KNOW WHY, BUT I FELT LIKE MY INSIDES WERE KNOTTING UP... IT'LL PASS, THOUGH!

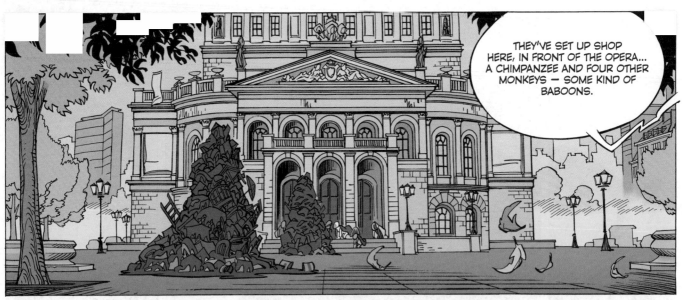

THEY'VE SET UP SHOP HERE, IN FRONT OF THE OPERA... A CHIMPANZEE AND FOUR OTHER MONKEYS — SOME KIND OF BABOONS.

AND ALL OF THEM IN COSTUMES?! THAT BURNED-OUT CIRCUS HADN'T GIVEN UP ALL OF ITS RESIDENTS YET...

THESE ARE DIFFERENT FROM THE OTHER ANIMALS. THERE'S SOMETHING WRONG WITH THEM.

THEIR EYES ARE WEIRD ... AND HAVE YOU SEEN HOW STILL THEY ARE? AS IF THEY WERE WAITING FOR SOMETHING...

AND THOSE PILES OF STUFF? IT MAKES NO SENSE!

THEY REMIND ME OF CAIRNS.

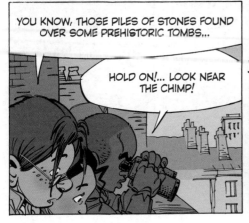

YOU KNOW, THOSE PILES OF STONES FOUND OVER SOME PREHISTORIC TOMBS...

HOLD ON!... LOOK NEAR THE CHIMP!

YEAH? SO?

AT THE FOOT OF THE COLUMN.

OH, CRAP! THE BABY'S THERE!

WAAAH
WAAAH

WAAAH!
WAAAH!

HEEAAA

WAAAH!
WAAAH!

THAT ONE'S GOING TO ATTACK THE BABY!

EXCEPT THE CHIMPANZEE WANTS TO KEEP HER FOR ITSELF!

HEEEAAGH! HEEEEEHH!

EEEEK! EEEEK!

IT'S TAKING HER INSIDE! WE'VE GOT TO DO SOMETHING!

DODZI! TELL US WHAT TO DO!

SHOOT THEM, DODZI!

I CAN'T!... I MIGHT HIT THE BABY!...

WE CAN'T LEAVE HER TO THEM — THEY'LL EAT HER FOR SURE!

SHE'S RIGHT. WE HAVE TO GO!

WAIT, NO, IT'S... IT'S NOT A GOOD IDEA... I DON'T WANT TO GO!

THEY... THEY'LL ATTACK US! AND A CHIMPANZEE'S AT LEAST THREE TIMES AS STRONG AS A MAN!... DIDN'T YOU SEE WHAT THEY DID TO THE MASTER OF KNIVES?

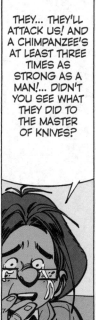

WHAT ELSE ARE WE SUPPOSED TO DO?

I DON'T KNOW!... WE HAVE TO THINK OF A PLAN!... GO BACK TO THE CIRCUS TO SEE WHAT YOU CAN LEARN ABOUT THEM! PLEASE!

STOP BEING AFRAID ALL THE TIME, WILL YOU?! WE'RE SICK OF IT, AND IT DOESN'T HELP!

19

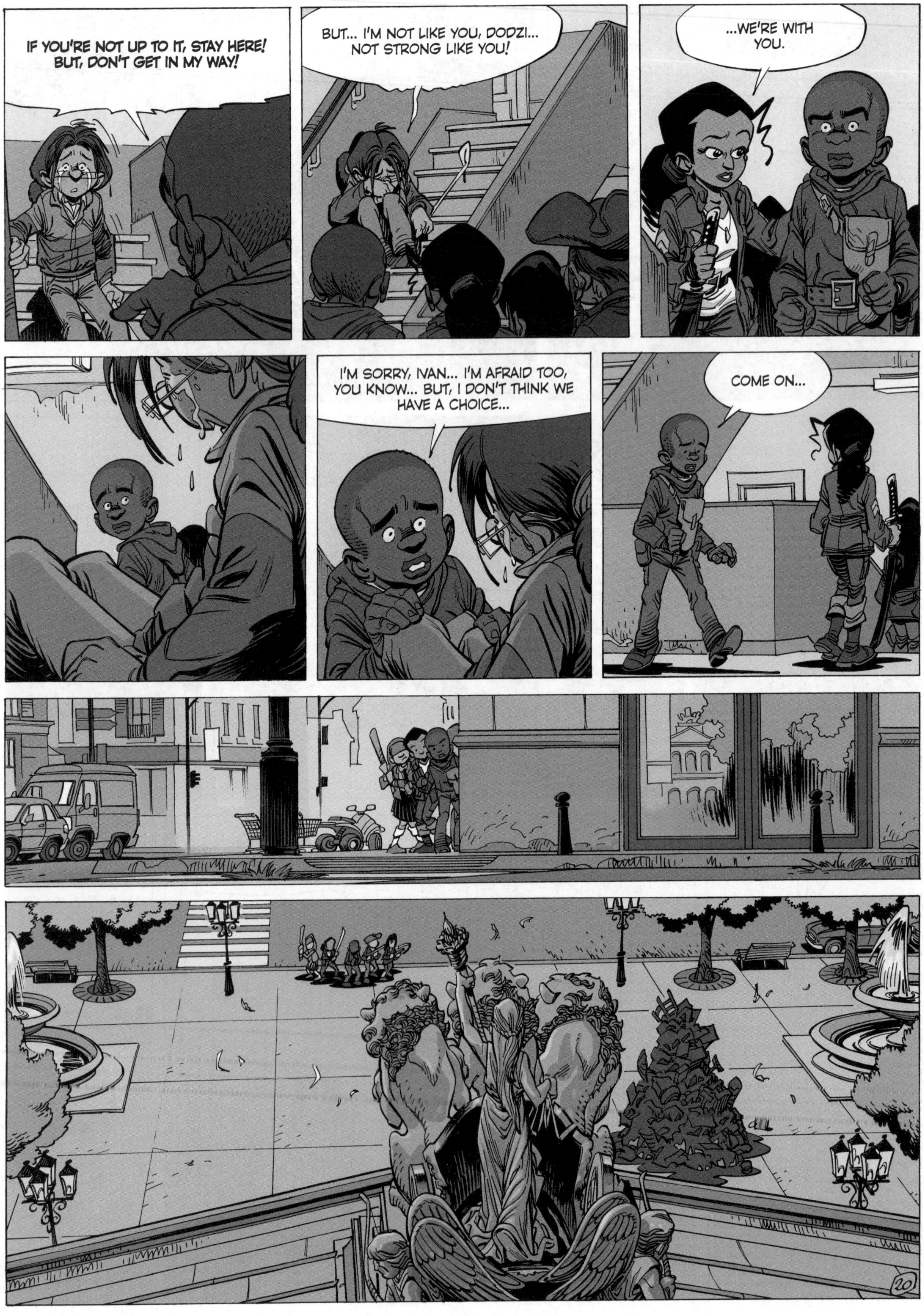
IF YOU'RE NOT UP TO IT, STAY HERE! BUT, DON'T GET IN MY WAY!
BUT... I'M NOT LIKE YOU, DODZI... NOT STRONG LIKE YOU!
...WE'RE WITH YOU.
I'M SORRY, IVAN... I'M AFRAID TOO, YOU KNOW... BUT, I DON'T THINK WE HAVE A CHOICE...
COME ON...
20

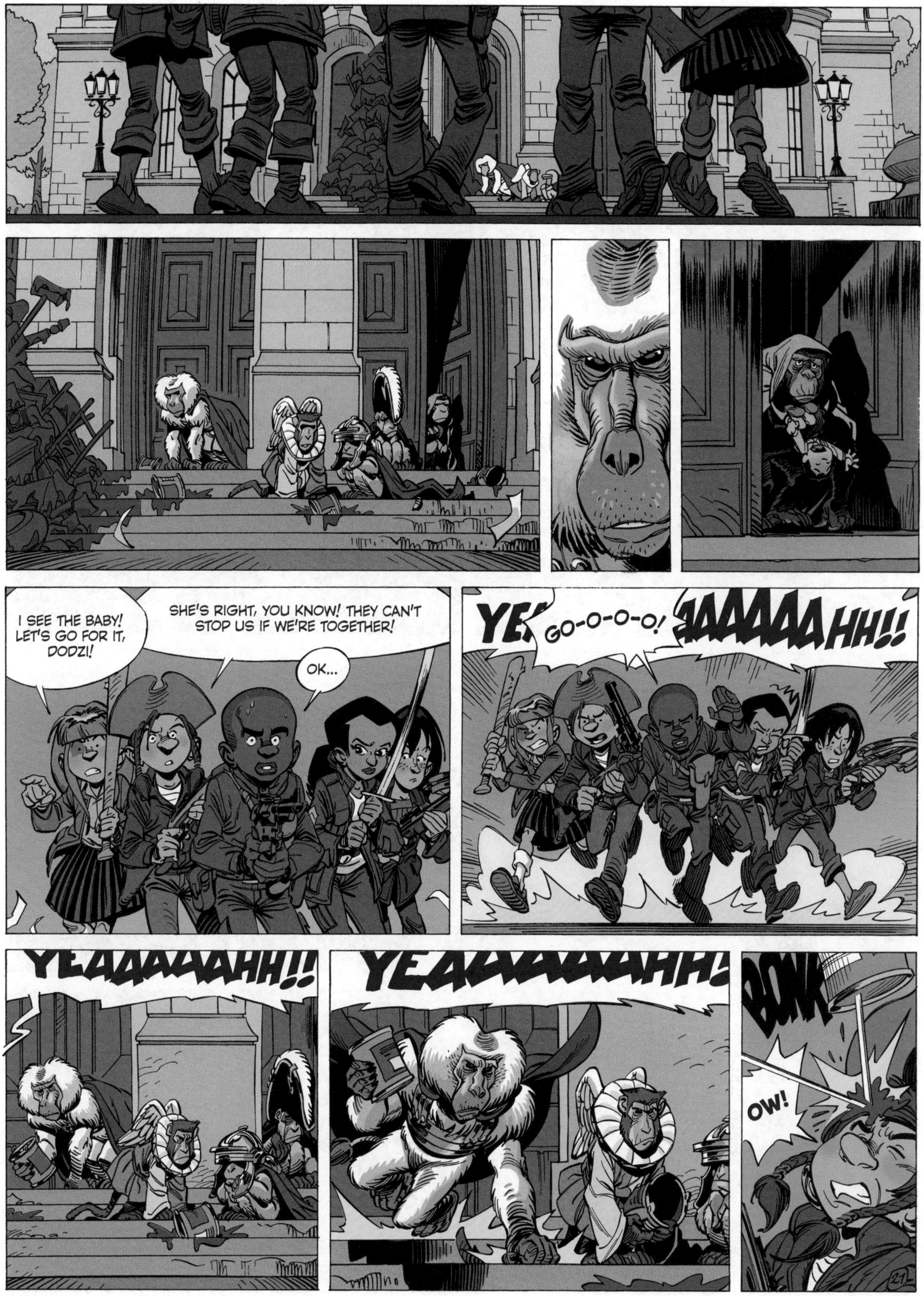

I SEE THE BABY! LET'S GO FOR IT, DODZI!
SHE'S RIGHT, YOU KNOW! THEY CAN'T STOP US IF WE'RE TOGETHER!
OK...
YEA
GO-O-O-O!
AAAAAAHH!!
YEAAAAAAHH!!
YEAAAAAAAHH!
BONK
OW!

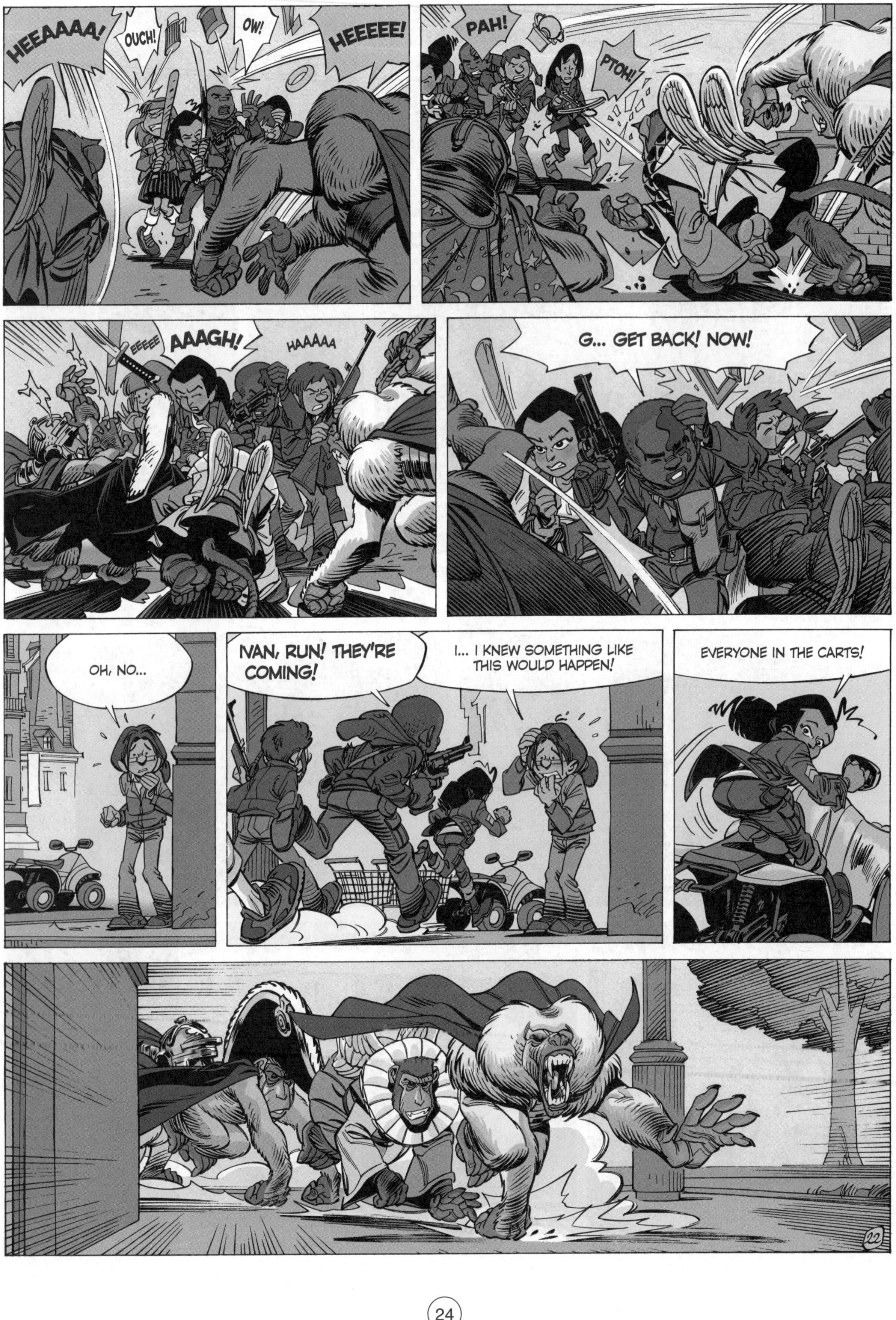
HEEAAAA!
OUCH!
OW!
HEEEEE!
PAH!
PTOH!
EEEEE
AAAGH!
HAAAAA
G... GET BACK! NOW!
OH, NO...
IVAN, RUN! THEY'RE COMING!
I... I KNEW SOMETHING LIKE THIS WOULD HAPPEN!
EVERYONE IN THE CARTS!
22

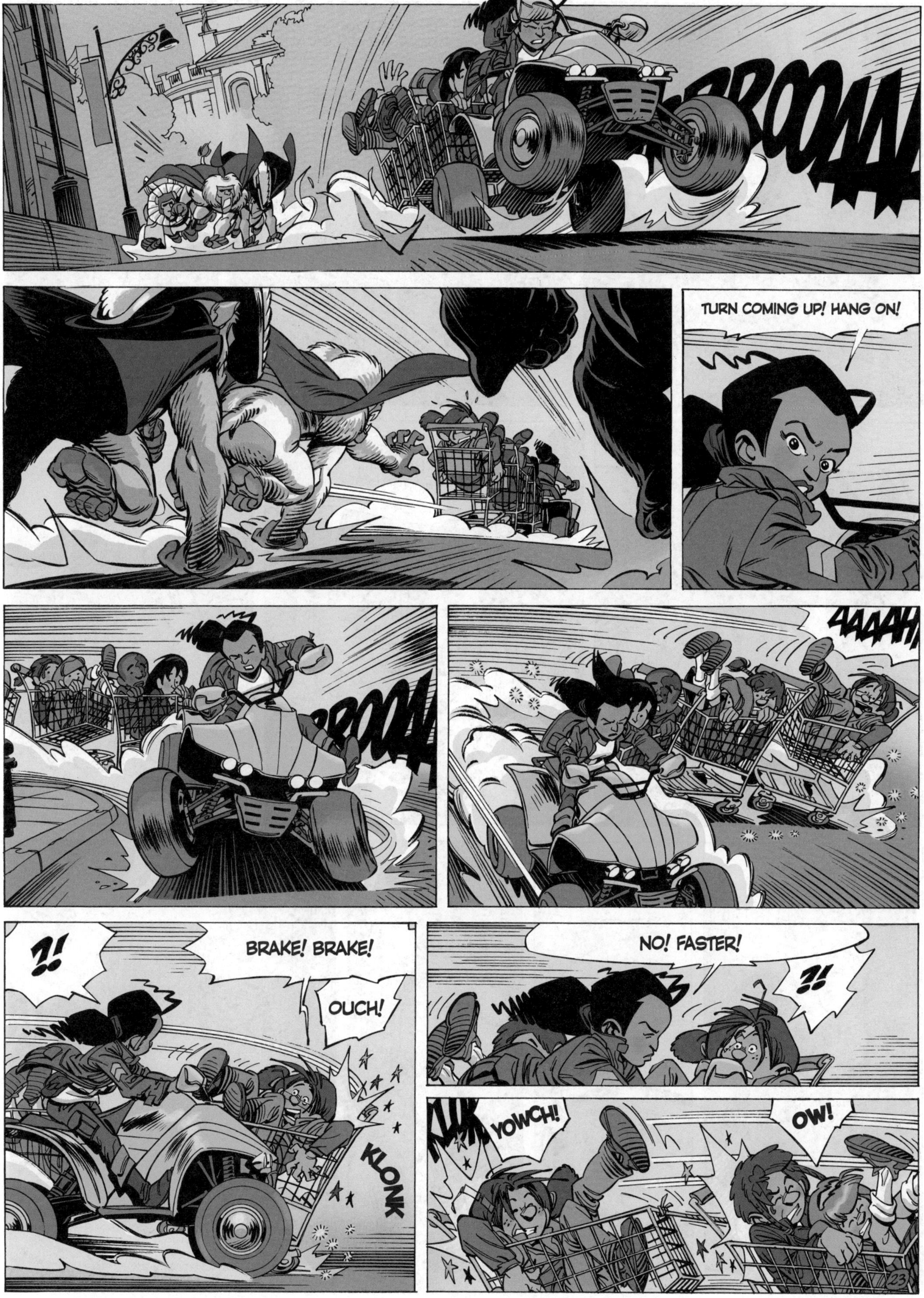

VRROOAAAM
TURN COMING UP! HANG ON!
VRROOAAM
AAAAH
?!
BRAKE! BRAKE!
OUCH!
KLONK
NO! FASTER!
?!
KLUK
YOWCH!
OW!

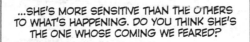
...SHE'S MORE SENSITIVE THAN THE OTHERS TO WHAT'S HAPPENING. DO YOU THINK SHE'S THE ONE WHOSE COMING WE FEARED?

YOU KNOW WE CAN'T TAKE ANY CHANCES.

LEAVE HER ALONE, MEANIE!

PAK

WHAT ARE YOU DOING TO CAMILLE?! IF YOU TOUCH HER, I'LL... I'LL BONK YOU ON THE HEAD!

MMHFF!?

STAY OUT OF THIS...

...YOU DON'T KNOW WHO YOU'RE DEALING WITH.

HEEEEEE... HEEEEE!

...WHAT'S GOING ON?

HEEEE... HEEEE!

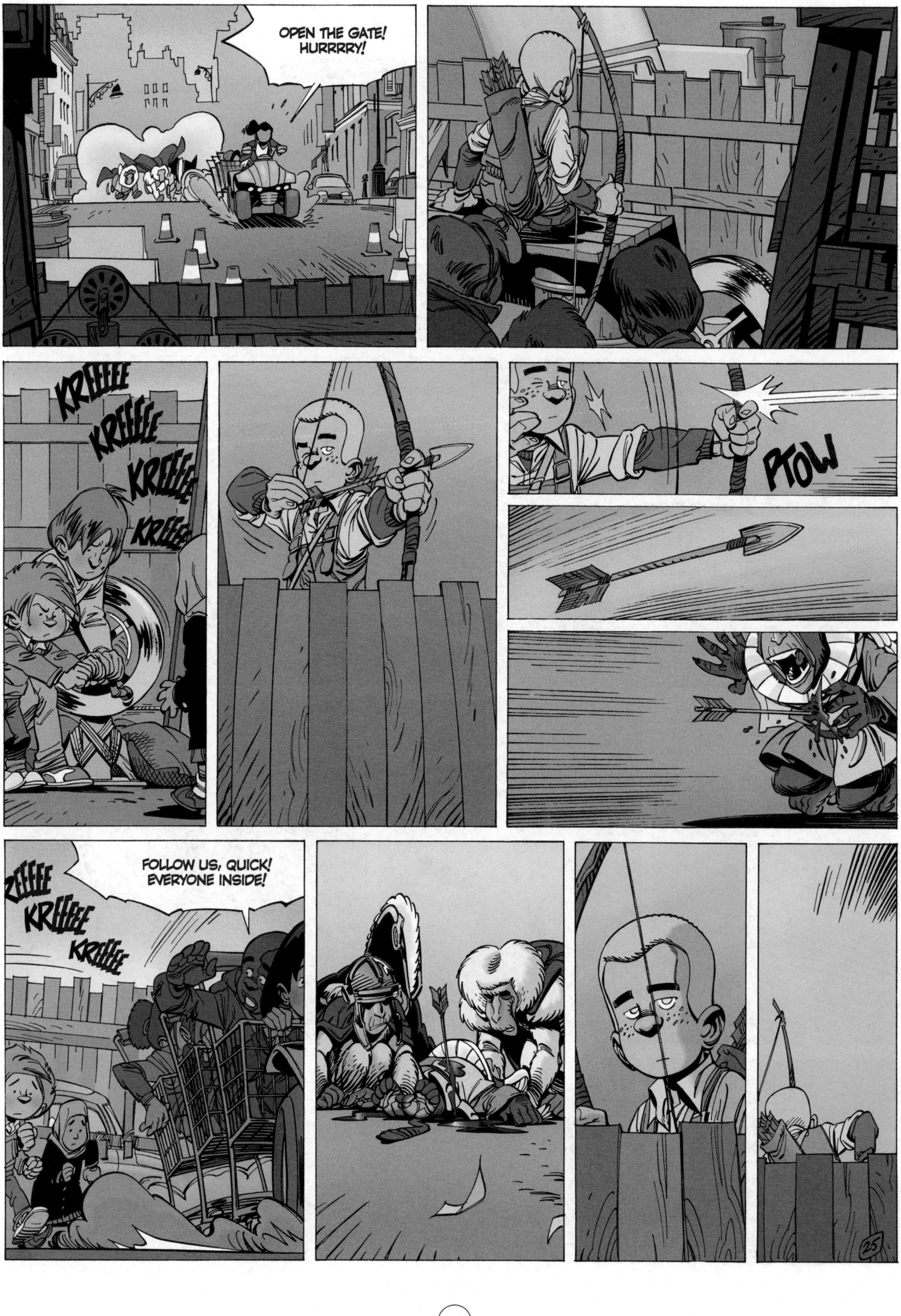
OPEN THE GATE!
HURRRRY!
KREEEEE
KREEEEE
KREEEEE
KREEEE
PTOW
FOLLOW US, QUICK!
EVERYONE INSIDE!
ZEEEEE
KREEEEE
KREEEE
25

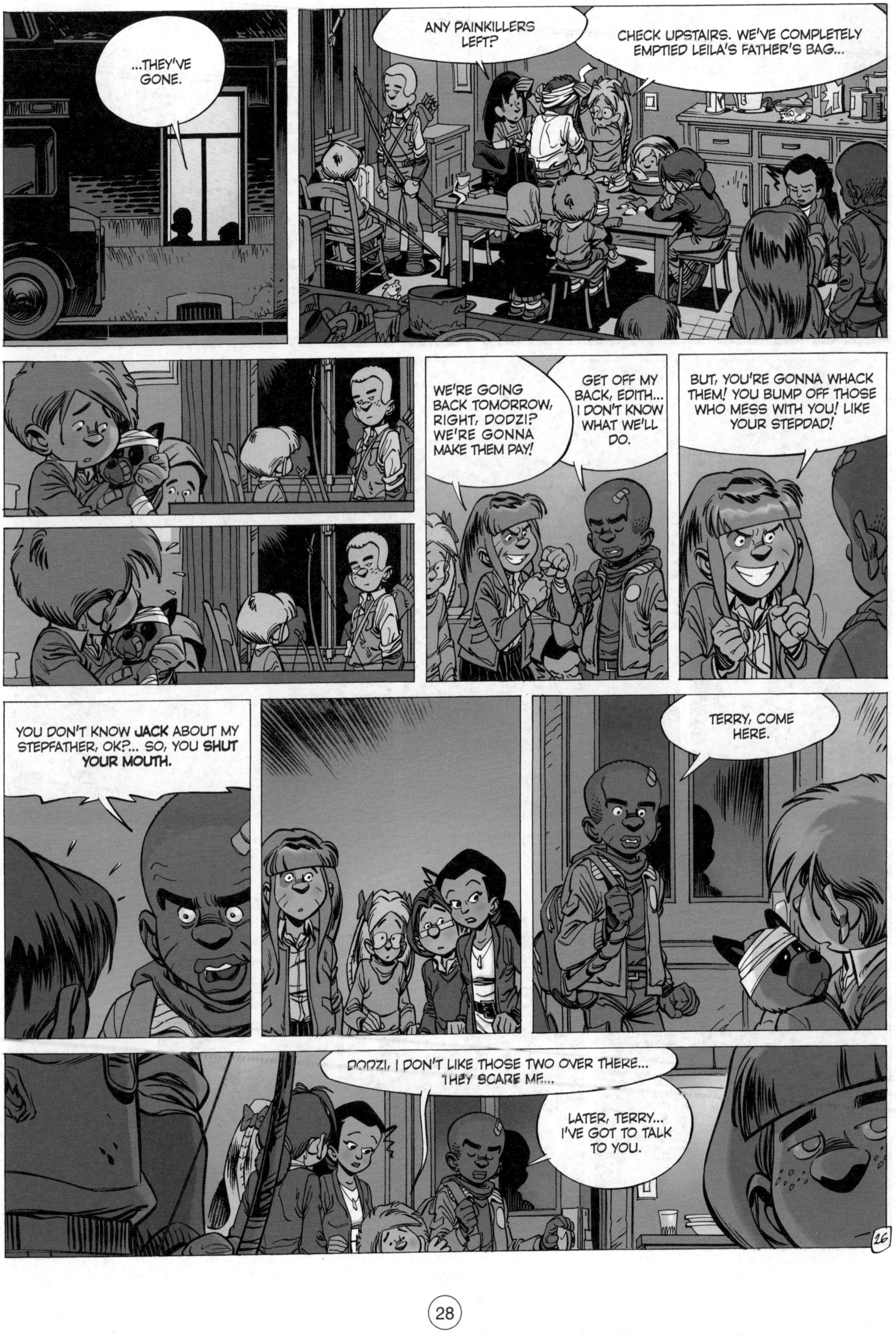
...THEY'VE GONE.
ANY PAINKILLERS LEFT?
CHECK UPSTAIRS. WE'VE COMPLETELY EMPTIED LEILA'S FATHER'S BAG...
WE'RE GOING BACK TOMORROW, RIGHT, DODZI? WE'RE GONNA MAKE THEM PAY!
GET OFF MY BACK, EDITH... I DON'T KNOW WHAT WE'LL DO.
BUT, YOU'RE GONNA WHACK THEM! YOU BUMP OFF THOSE WHO MESS WITH YOU! LIKE YOUR STEPDAD!
YOU DON'T KNOW JACK ABOUT MY STEPFATHER, OK?... SO, YOU SHUT YOUR MOUTH.
TERRY, COME HERE.
DODZI, I DON'T LIKE THOSE TWO OVER THERE... THEY SCARE ME...
LATER, TERRY... I'VE GOT TO TALK TO YOU.
26

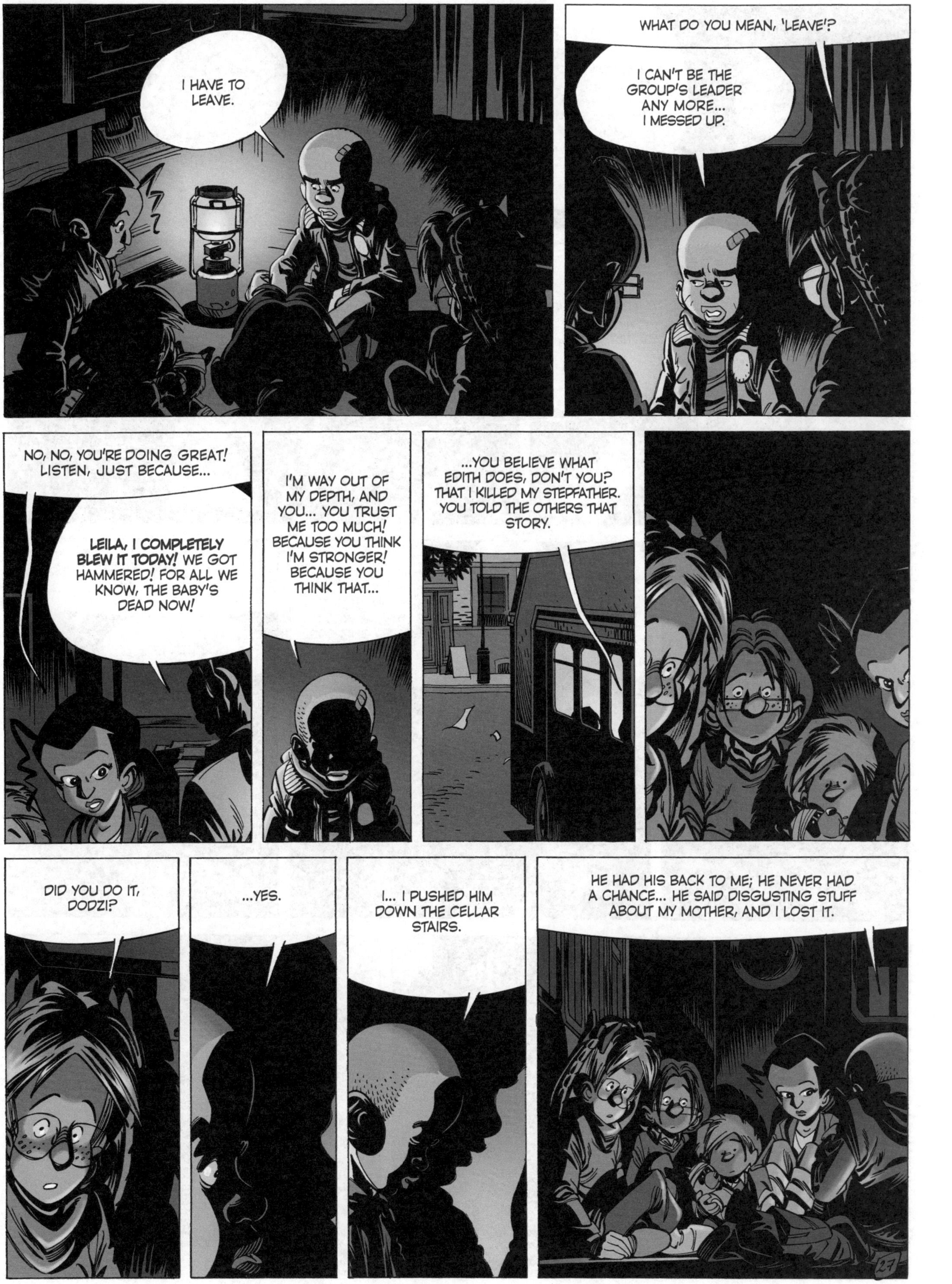

I HAVE TO LEAVE.
WHAT DO YOU MEAN, 'LEAVE'?
I CAN'T BE THE GROUP'S LEADER ANY MORE... I MESSED UP.
NO, NO, YOU'RE DOING GREAT! LISTEN, JUST BECAUSE...
LEILA, I COMPLETELY BLEW IT TODAY! WE GOT HAMMERED! FOR ALL WE KNOW, THE BABY'S DEAD NOW!
I'M WAY OUT OF MY DEPTH, AND YOU... YOU TRUST ME TOO MUCH! BECAUSE YOU THINK I'M STRONGER! BECAUSE YOU THINK THAT...
...YOU BELIEVE WHAT EDITH DOES, DON'T YOU? THAT I KILLED MY STEPFATHER. YOU TOLD THE OTHERS THAT STORY.
DID YOU DO IT, DODZI?
...YES.
I... I PUSHED HIM DOWN THE CELLAR STAIRS.
HE HAD HIS BACK TO ME; HE NEVER HAD A CHANCE... HE SAID DISGUSTING STUFF ABOUT MY MOTHER, AND I LOST IT.

BUT, IT'S EATING AT ME, YOU UNDERSTAND?... THE MORE YOU LOOK AT ME AS IF I WERE COOL, AS IF I WERE SOME SORT OF HERO, THE MORE IT EATS AT ME...

...I DON'T WANT TO TELL THE OTHERS... IT'S NONE OF THEIR BUSINESS.

THAT'S WHY I HAVE TO LEAVE. YOU'LL DO BETTER WITHOUT ME.

IVAN, YOU'LL BE THE LEADER WHILE I'M GONE.

WHAT?!

YOU WERE RIGHT, EARLIER. WE SHOULD HAVE LISTENED TO YOU. SO, IT'S UP TO YOU TO SOLVE THE BABY SITUATION.

ER... ARE YOU SURE ABOUT THIS, DODZI?

BUT, I... I'M NOT CAPABLE OF...

I'M SURE YOU'LL RISE TO THE OCCASION. BESIDES, THE OTHERS WILL BE THERE TO SUPPORT YOU.

AND I'LL NEVER BE TOO FAR, ALL RIGHT?

YOU PROMISE?

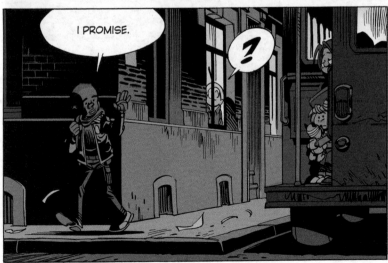

I PROMISE.

?

HEY... WHERE'S DODZI GOING?

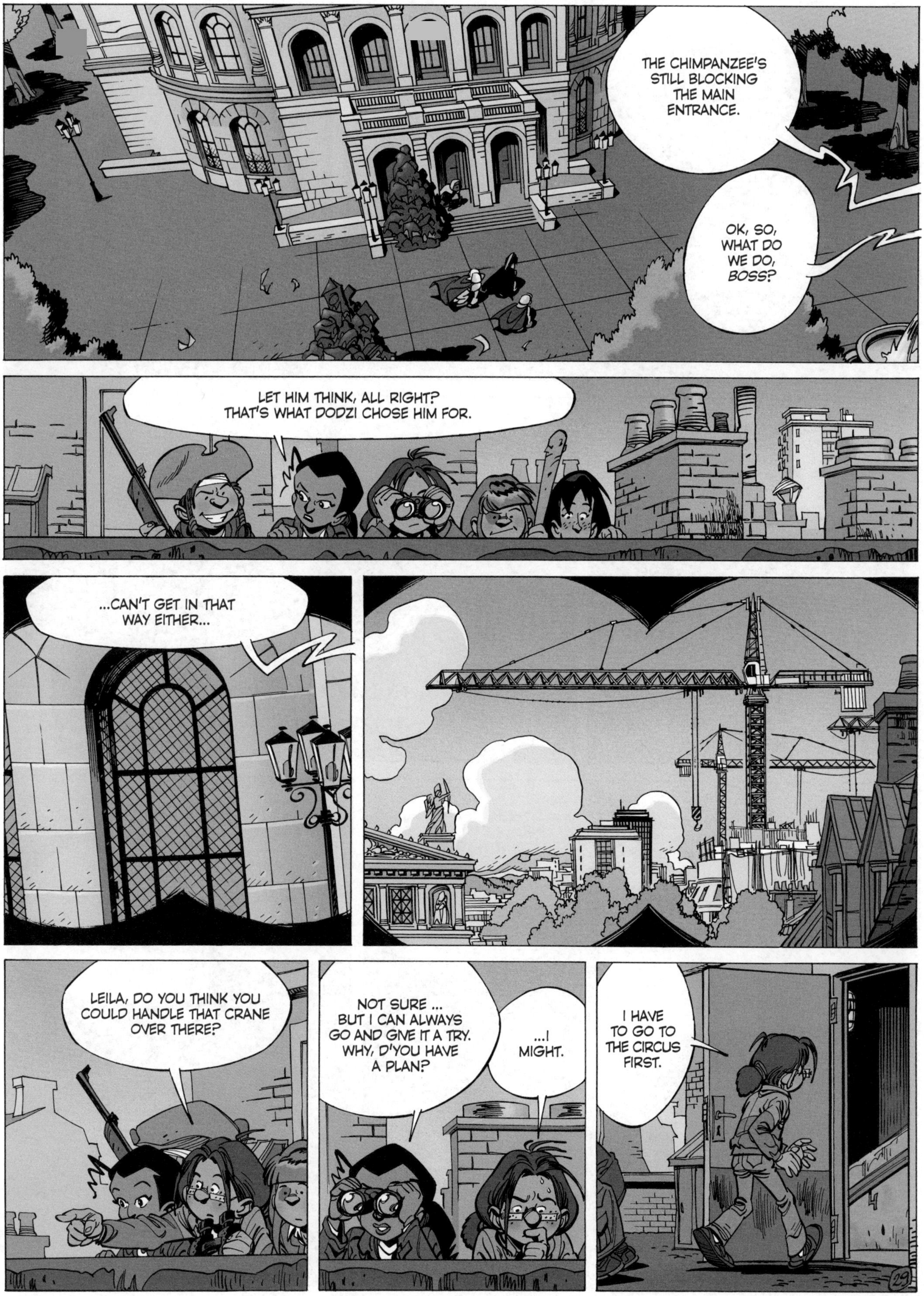
THE CHIMPANZEE'S STILL BLOCKING THE MAIN ENTRANCE.
OK, SO, WHAT DO WE DO, *BOSS*?
LET HIM THINK, ALL RIGHT? THAT'S WHAT DODZI CHOSE HIM FOR.
...CAN'T GET IN THAT WAY EITHER...
LEILA, DO YOU THINK YOU COULD HANDLE THAT CRANE OVER THERE?
NOT SURE ... BUT I CAN ALWAYS GO AND GIVE IT A TRY. WHY, D'YOU HAVE A PLAN?
...I MIGHT.
I HAVE TO GO TO THE CIRCUS FIRST.
29

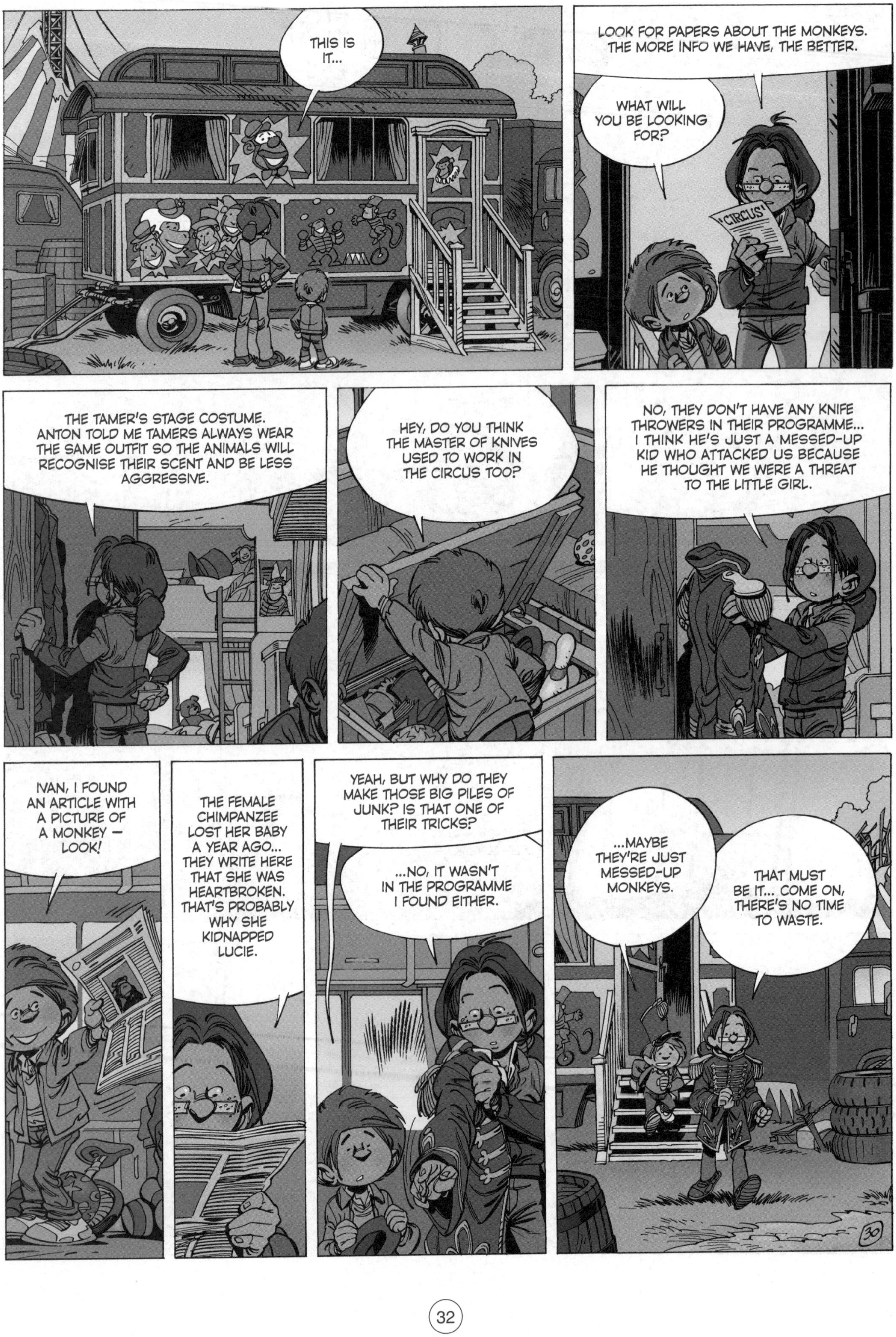
THIS IS IT...
LOOK FOR PAPERS ABOUT THE MONKEYS. THE MORE INFO WE HAVE, THE BETTER.
WHAT WILL YOU BE LOOKING FOR?
CIRCUS!
THE TAMER'S STAGE COSTUME. ANTON TOLD ME TAMERS ALWAYS WEAR THE SAME OUTFIT SO THE ANIMALS WILL RECOGNISE THEIR SCENT AND BE LESS AGGRESSIVE.
HEY, DO YOU THINK THE MASTER OF KNIVES USED TO WORK IN THE CIRCUS TOO?
NO, THEY DON'T HAVE ANY KNIFE THROWERS IN THEIR PROGRAMME... I THINK HE'S JUST A MESSED-UP KID WHO ATTACKED US BECAUSE HE THOUGHT WE WERE A THREAT TO THE LITTLE GIRL.
IVAN, I FOUND AN ARTICLE WITH A PICTURE OF A MONKEY — LOOK!
THE FEMALE CHIMPANZEE LOST HER BABY A YEAR AGO... THEY WRITE HERE THAT SHE WAS HEARTBROKEN. THAT'S PROBABLY WHY SHE KIDNAPPED LUCIE.
YEAH, BUT WHY DO THEY MAKE THOSE BIG PILES OF JUNK? IS THAT ONE OF THEIR TRICKS?
...NO, IT WASN'T IN THE PROGRAMME I FOUND EITHER.
...MAYBE THEY'RE JUST MESSED-UP MONKEYS.
THAT MUST BE IT... COME ON, THERE'S NO TIME TO WASTE.
30

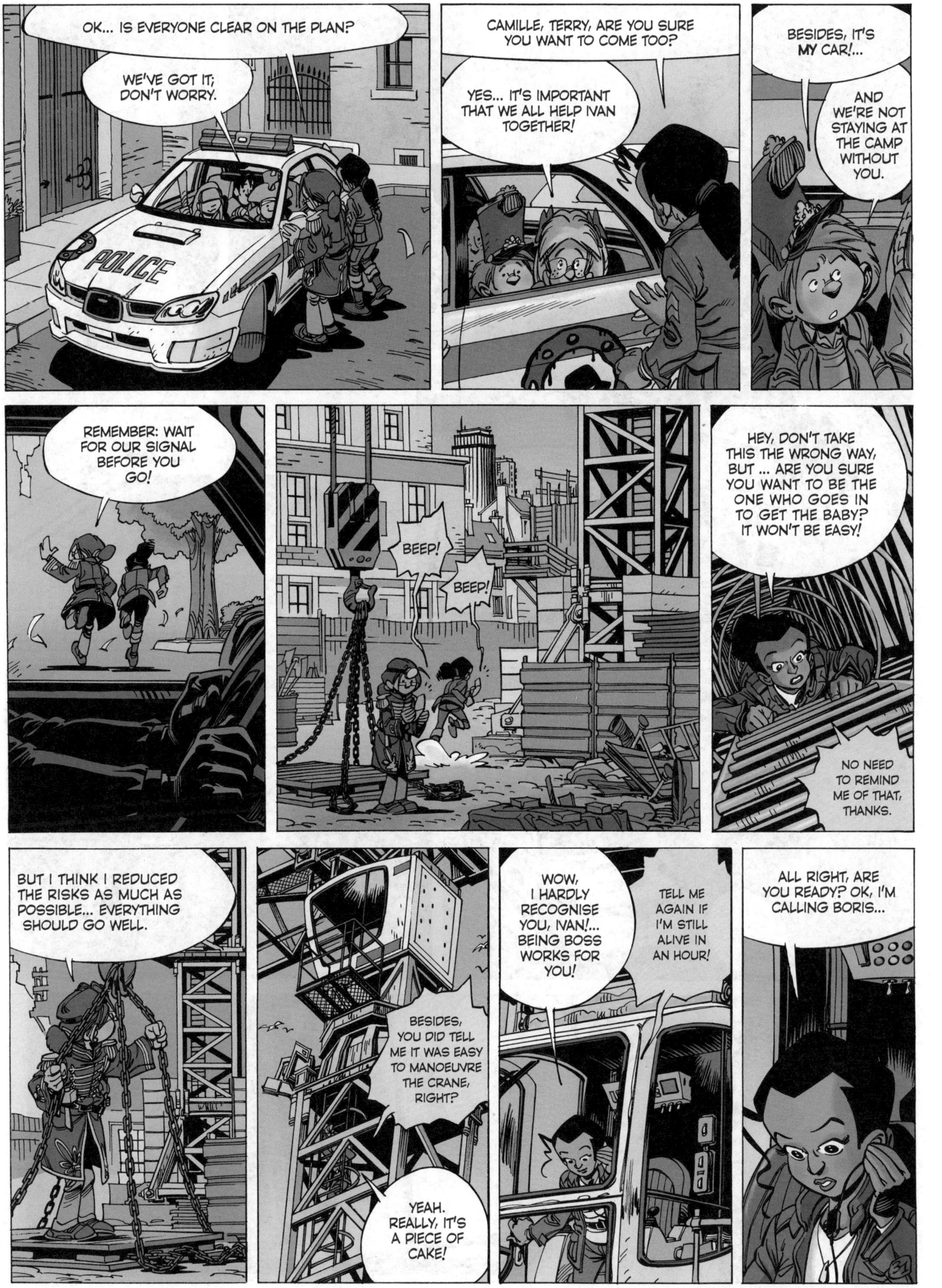

OK... IS EVERYONE CLEAR ON THE PLAN?
WE'VE GOT IT; DON'T WORRY.
POLICE
CAMILLE, TERRY, ARE YOU SURE YOU WANT TO COME TOO?
YES... IT'S IMPORTANT THAT WE ALL HELP IVAN TOGETHER!
BESIDES, IT'S MY CAR!...
AND WE'RE NOT STAYING AT THE CAMP WITHOUT YOU.
REMEMBER: WAIT FOR OUR SIGNAL BEFORE YOU GO!
BEEP!
BEEP!
HEY, DON'T TAKE THIS THE WRONG WAY, BUT ... ARE YOU SURE YOU WANT TO BE THE ONE WHO GOES IN TO GET THE BABY? IT WON'T BE EASY!
NO NEED TO REMIND ME OF THAT, THANKS.
BUT I THINK I REDUCED THE RISKS AS MUCH AS POSSIBLE... EVERYTHING SHOULD GO WELL.
BESIDES, YOU DID TELL ME IT WAS EASY TO MANOEUVRE THE CRANE, RIGHT?
YEAH. REALLY, IT'S A PIECE OF CAKE!
WOW, I HARDLY RECOGNISE YOU, IVAN!... BEING BOSS WORKS FOR YOU!
TELL ME AGAIN IF I'M STILL ALIVE IN AN HOUR!
ALL RIGHT, ARE YOU READY? OK, I'M CALLING BORIS...

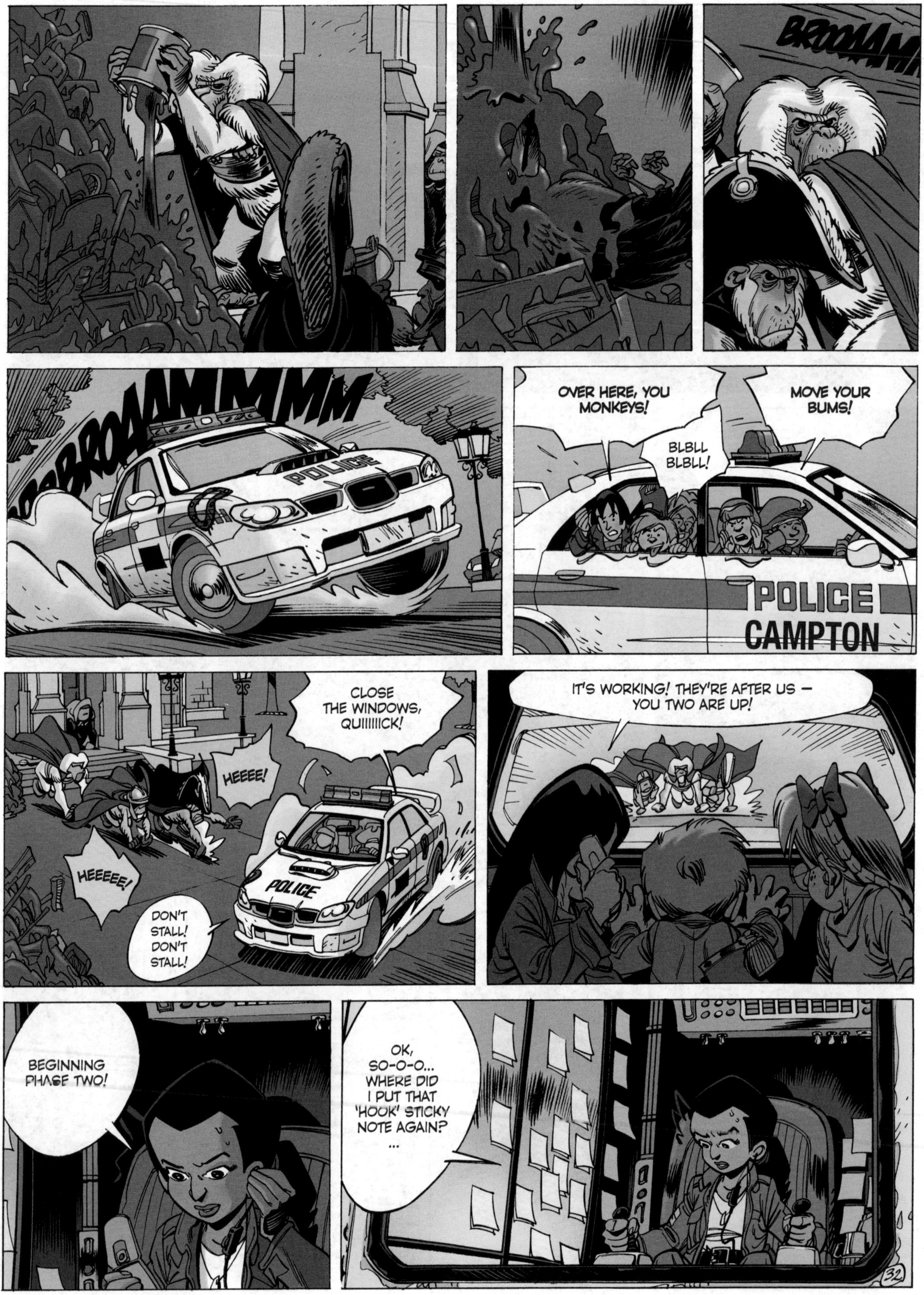
BROOAAMM
BROAAMMMMM
OVER HERE, YOU MONKEYS!
BLBLL BLBLL!
MOVE YOUR BUMS!
CLOSE THE WINDOWS, QUIIIIIICK!
HEEEE!
HEEEEE!
DON'T STALL! DON'T STALL!
IT'S WORKING! THEY'RE AFTER US – YOU TWO ARE UP!
BEGINNING PHASE TWO!
OK, SO-O-O... WHERE DID I PUT THAT 'HOOK' STICKY NOTE AGAIN? ...

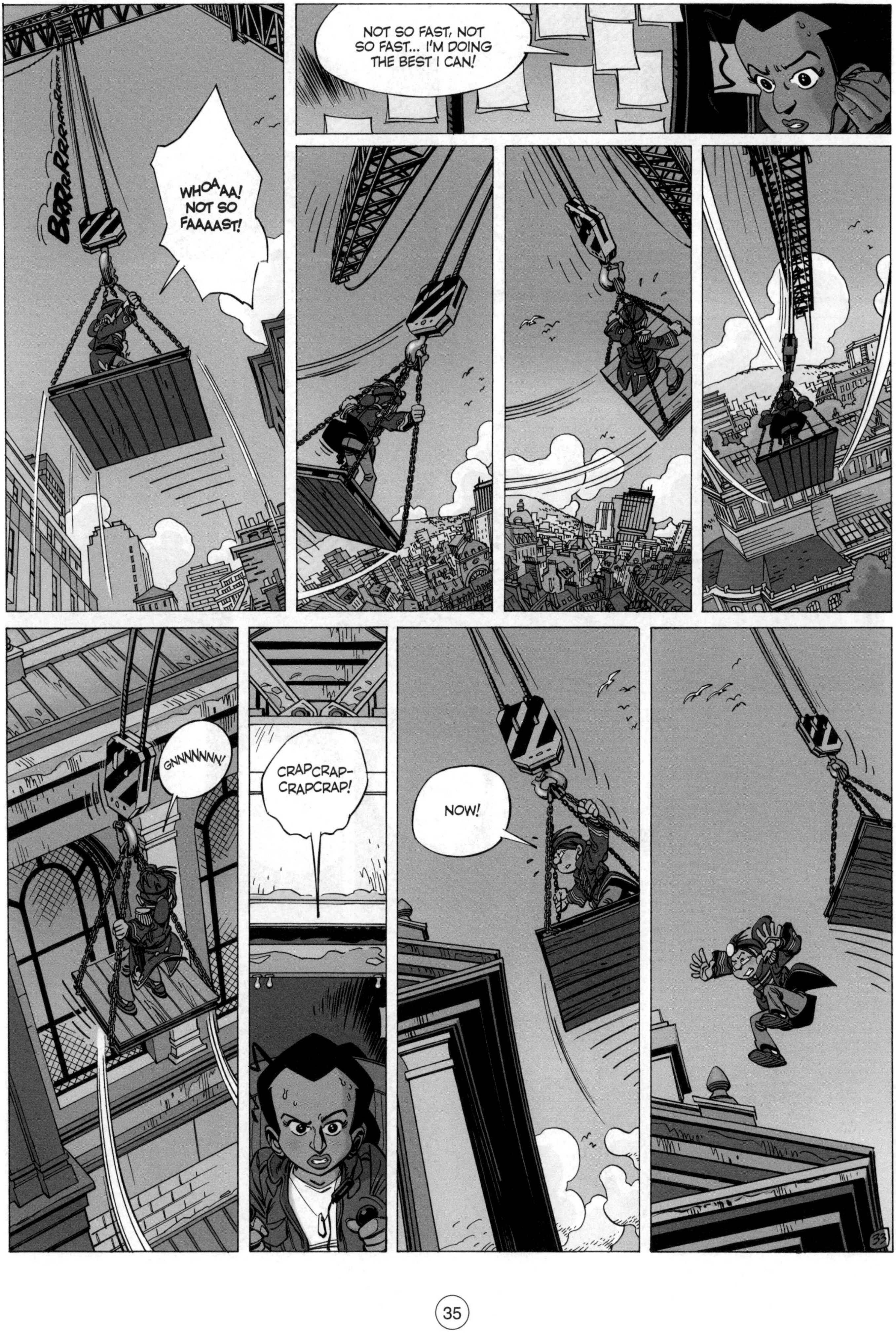
BRRRRRRRRRRRRRRR
WHOAAA! NOT SO FAAAAST!
NOT SO FAST, NOT SO FAST... I'M DOING THE BEST I CAN!
GNNNNNNN!
CRAPCRAP-CRAPCRAP!
NOW!

OW!...

IVAN, YOU OK?!

A PIECE OF CAKE, YOU SAID!? I'M NEVER EATING A CAKE YOU BAKE!

SKLANG

OH, MAN... IT'S SUPER SCARY IN THERE, LEILA!!... I DON'T WANT TO GO IN...

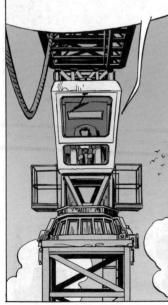

YOU **HAVE** TO KEEP GOING, IVAN. WE'VE GOT NO CHOICE NOW!... IN THE MEANTIME, I'LL BRING THE PLATFORM BACK TO THE ROOF; THAT WAY, YOU'LL BE ABLE TO LEAVE WHENEVER YOU WANT, OK?

LEILA?... HELLO, LEILA?!

OH, DEAR...

HHHHH...

...PHHEWWW!

34

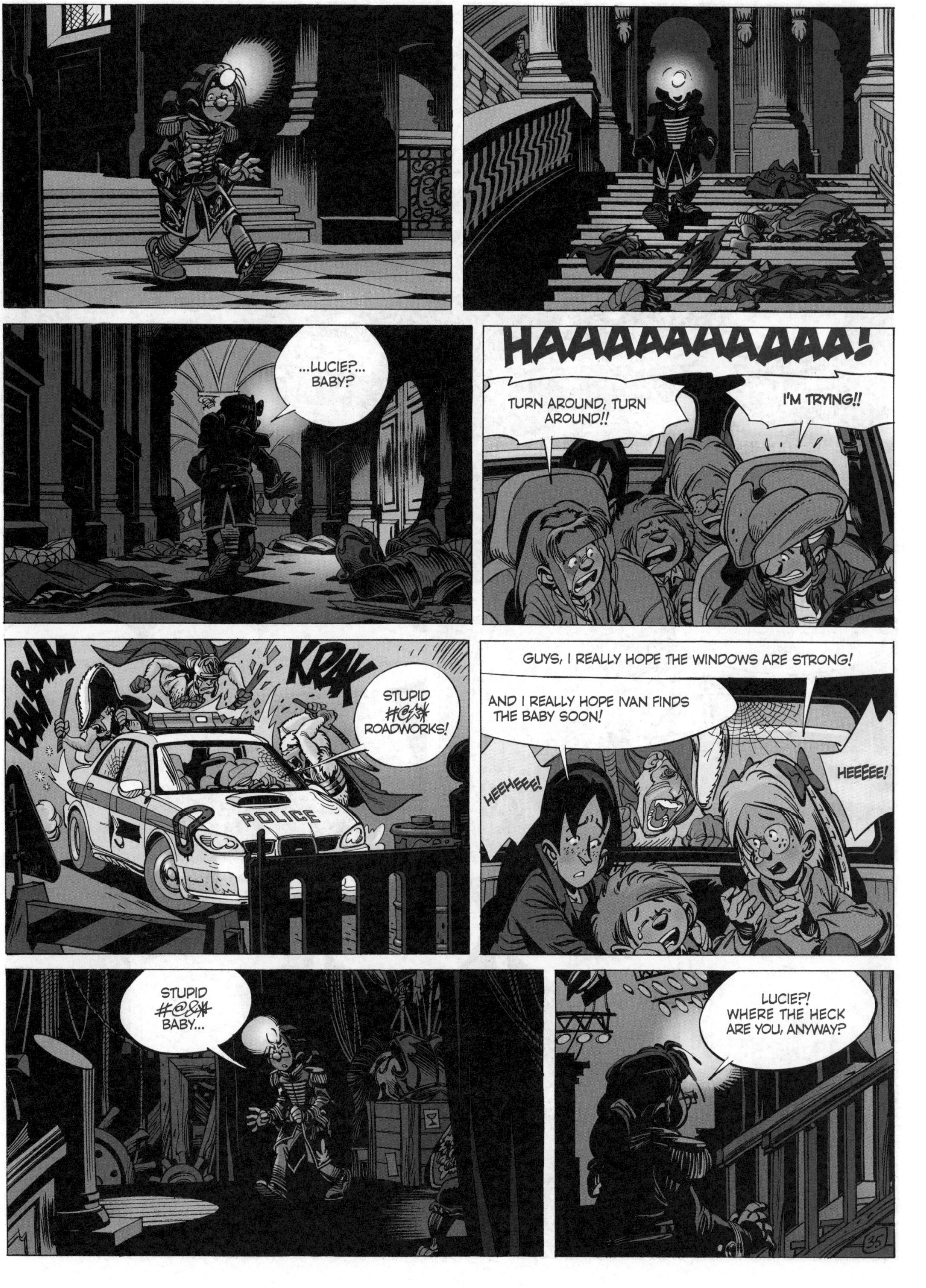
...LUCIE?... BABY?
HAAAAAAAAAAA!
TURN AROUND, TURN AROUND!!
I'M TRYING!!
BAM BAM
KRAK
STUPID #@&$ ROADWORKS!
POLICE
GUYS, I REALLY HOPE THE WINDOWS ARE STRONG!
AND I REALLY HOPE IVAN FINDS THE BABY SOON!
HEEHEEE!
HEEEEE!
STUPID #@&$ BABY...
LUCIE?! WHERE THE HECK ARE YOU, ANYWAY?

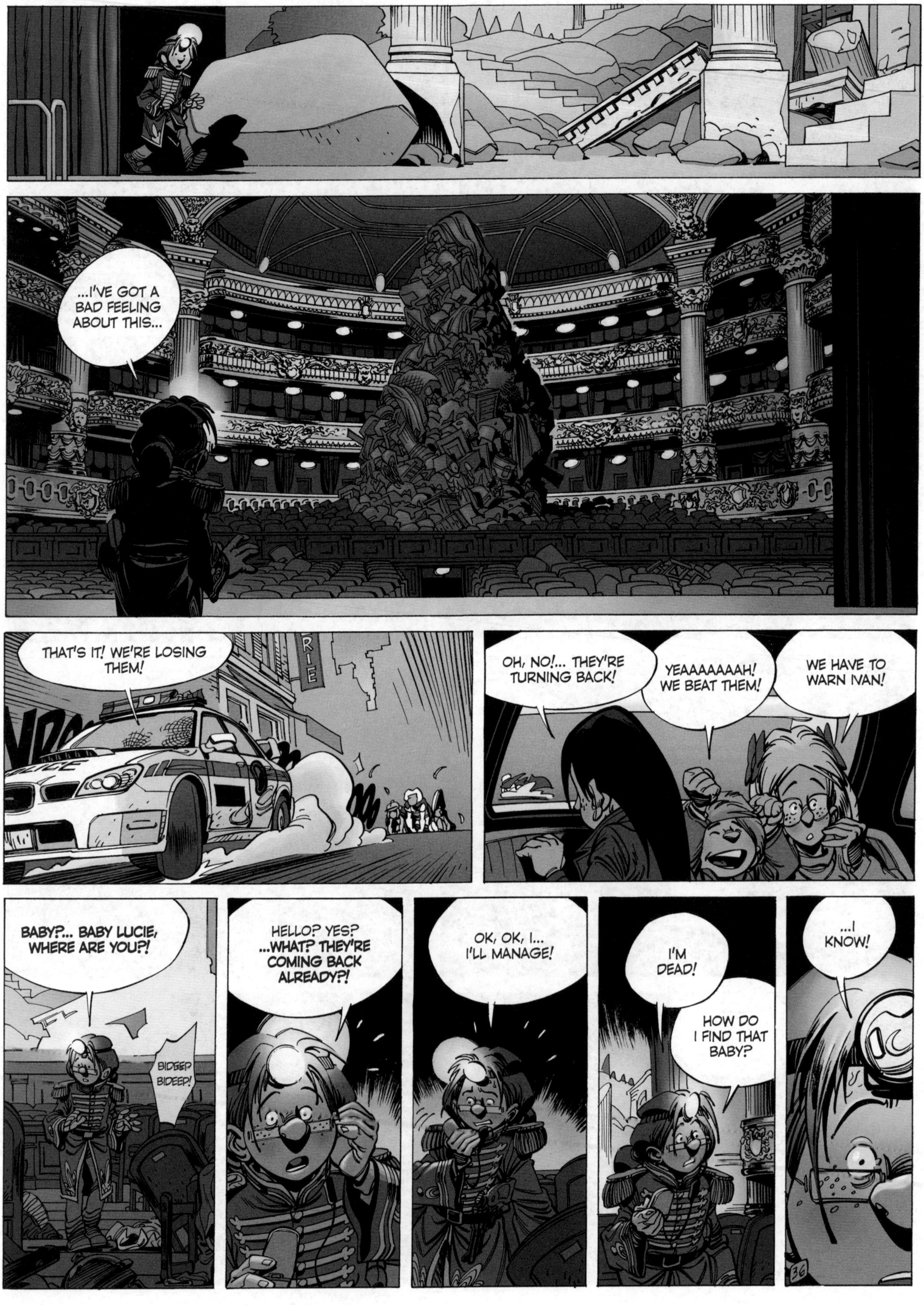
...I'VE GOT A BAD FEELING ABOUT THIS...
THAT'S IT! WE'RE LOSING THEM!
OH, NO!... THEY'RE TURNING BACK!
YEAAAAAAAH! WE BEAT THEM!
WE HAVE TO WARN IVAN!
BABY?... BABY LUCIE, WHERE ARE YOU?!
BIDEEP BIDEEP!
HELLO? YES? ...WHAT? THEY'RE COMING BACK ALREADY?!
OK, OK, I... I'LL MANAGE!
I'M DEAD!
HOW DO I FIND THAT BABY?
...I KNOW!

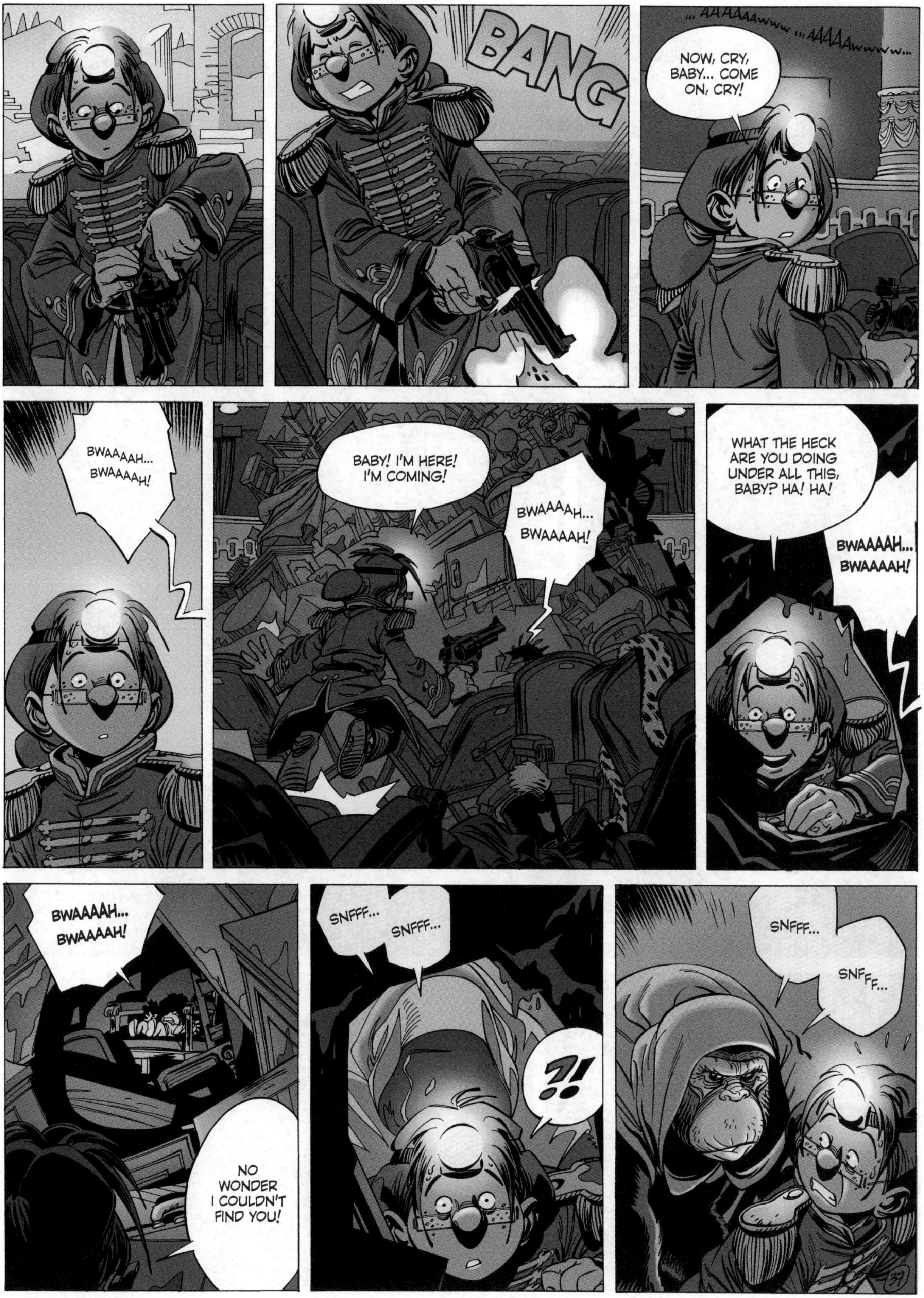

BANG
... AAAAAAwww ... AAAAAwwww...
NOW, CRY, BABY... COME ON, CRY!
BWAAAAH... BWAAAAH!
BABY! I'M HERE! I'M COMING!
BWAAAAH... BWAAAAH!
WHAT THE HECK ARE YOU DOING UNDER ALL THIS, BABY? HA! HA!
BWAAAAH... BWAAAAH!
BWAAAAH... BWAAAAH!
NO WONDER I COULDN'T FIND YOU!
SNFFF... SNFFF...
?!
SNFFF...
SNFFF...

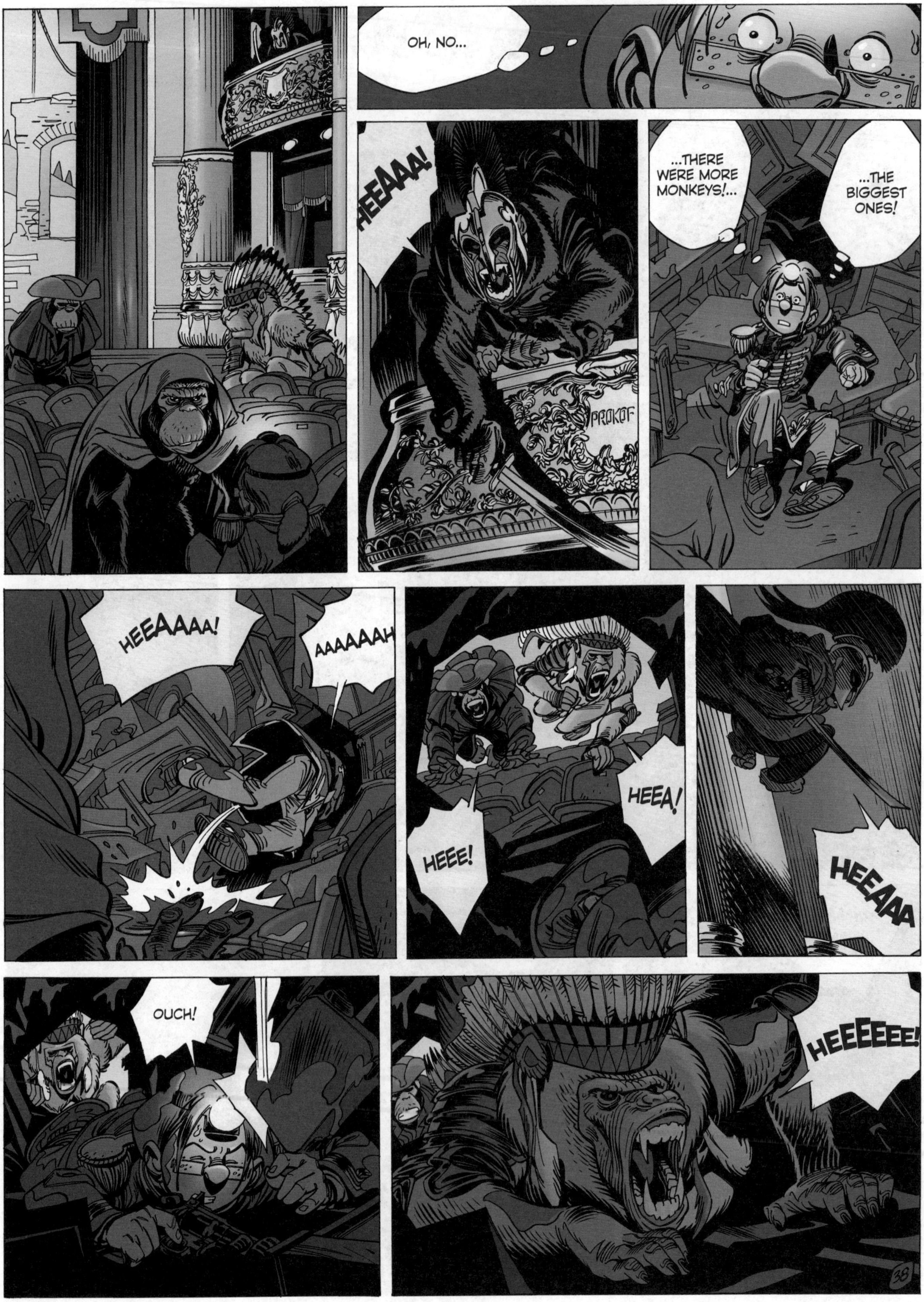
OH, NO...
HEEAAA!
...THERE WERE MORE MONKEYS!...
...THE BIGGEST ONES!
HEEAAAA!
AAAAAAH
HEEA!
HEEE!
HEEAAA
OUCH!
HEEEEEE!

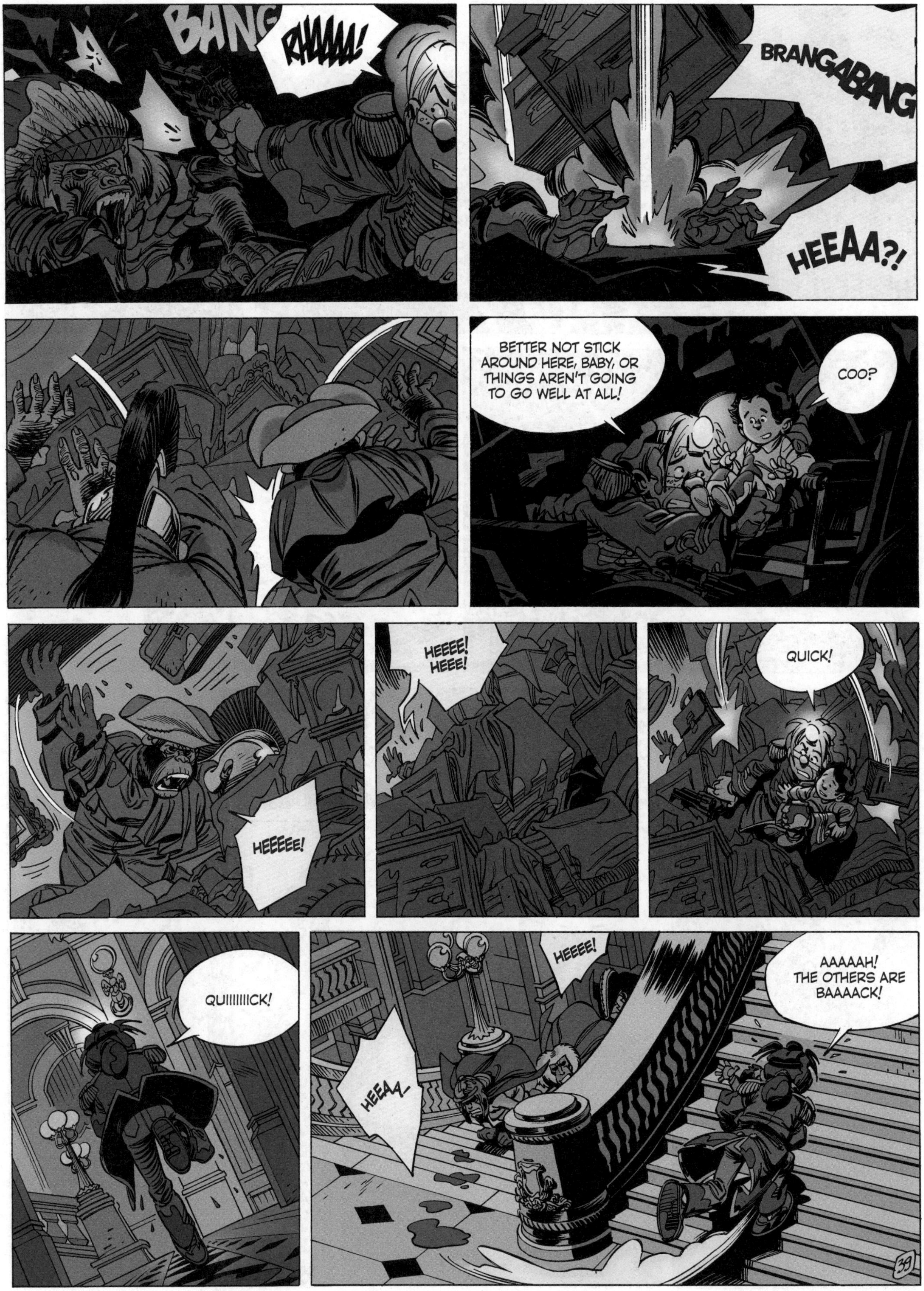
BANG
RHAAAA!
BRANGABANG
HEEAA?!
BETTER NOT STICK AROUND HERE, BABY, OR THINGS AREN'T GOING TO GO WELL AT ALL!
COO?
HEEEEE!
HEEEE! HEEE!
QUICK!
QUIIIIIIICK!
HEEEE!
HEEAA!
AAAAAH! THE OTHERS ARE BAAAACK!
39

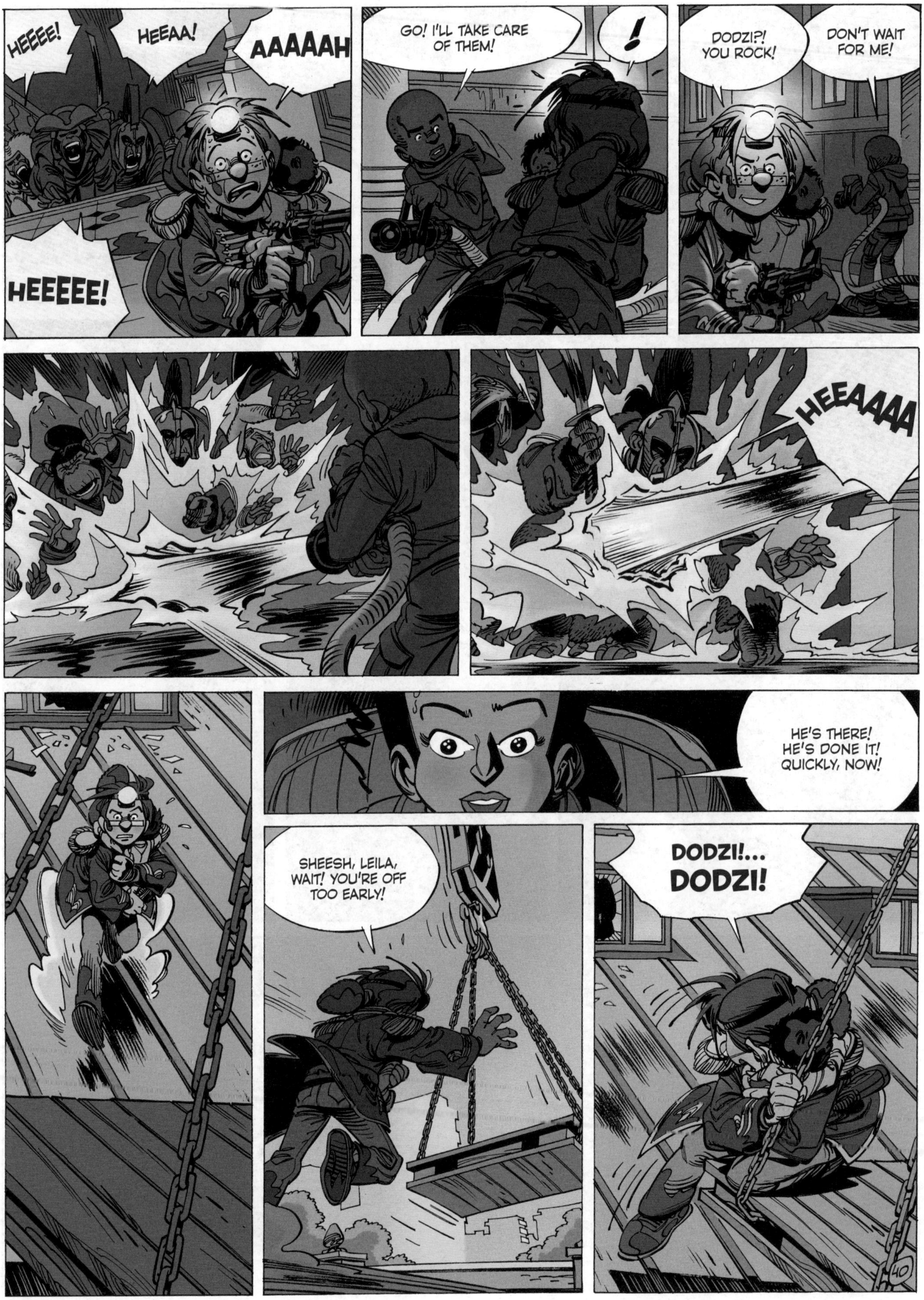
HEEEE!
HEEAA!
AAAAAH
HEEEEE!
GO! I'LL TAKE CARE OF THEM!
!
DODZI?! YOU ROCK!
DON'T WAIT FOR ME!
HEEAAAA
HE'S THERE! HE'S DONE IT! QUICKLY, NOW!
SHEESH, LEILA, WAIT! YOU'RE OFF TOO EARLY!
DODZI!... DODZI!
40

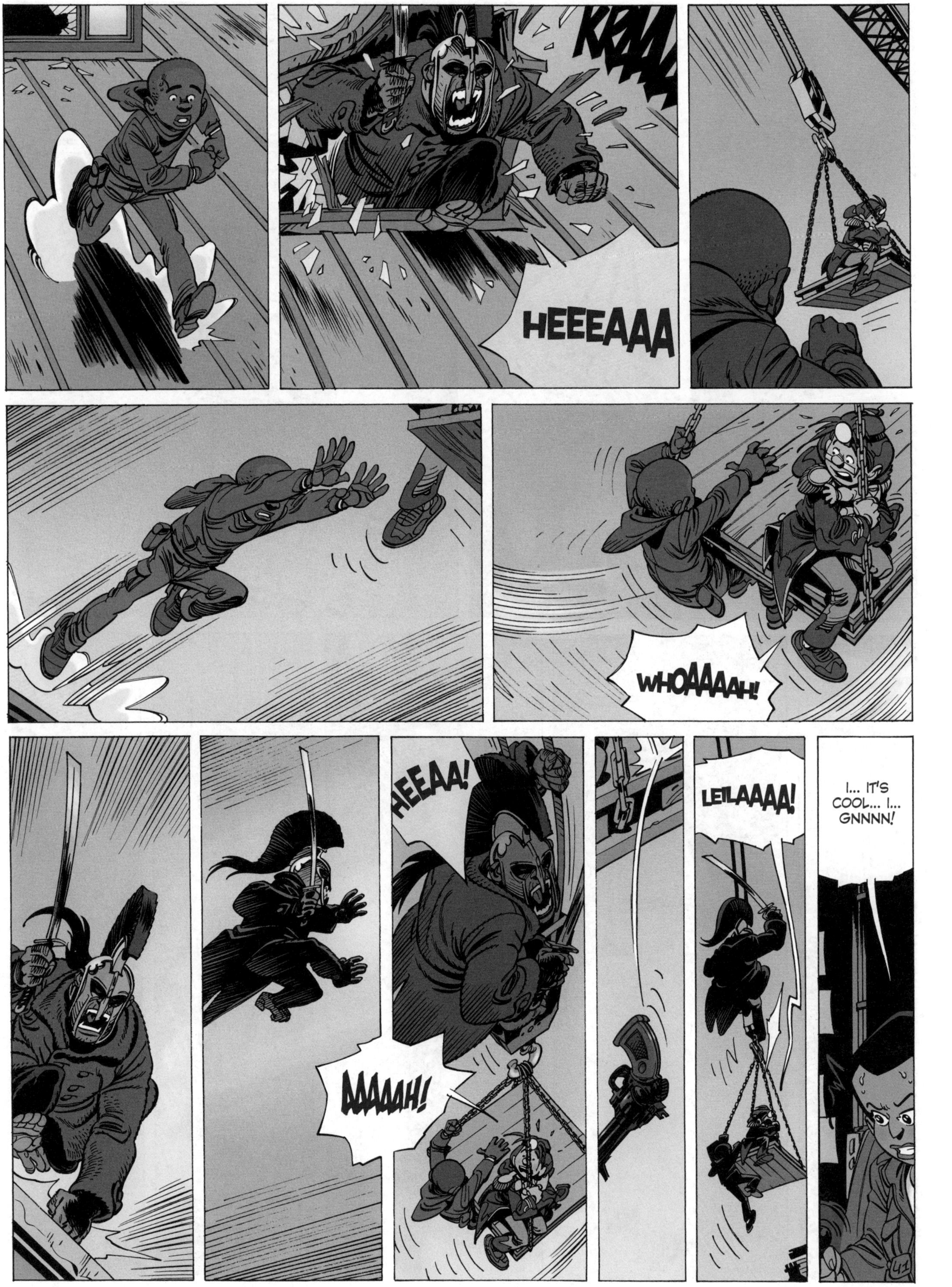
KRAAA
HEEEAAA
WHOAAAAH!
HEEAA!
AAAAAH!
LEILAAAA!
I... IT'S COOL... I... GNNNN!

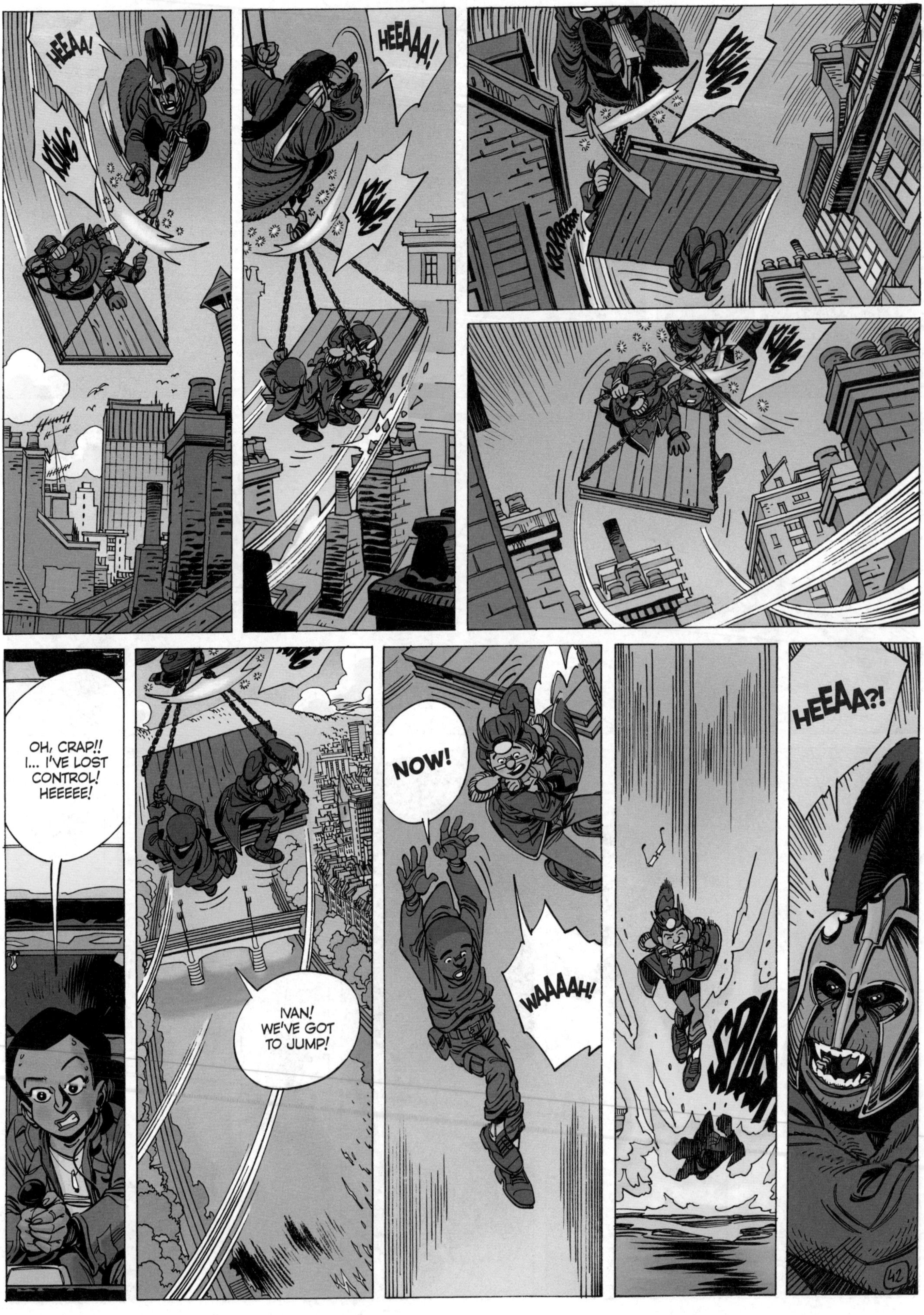
HEEAA!
HEEAAA!
OH, CRAP!! I... I'VE LOST CONTROL! HEEEEE!
IVAN! WE'VE GOT TO JUMP!
NOW!
WAAAAH!
HEEAA?!

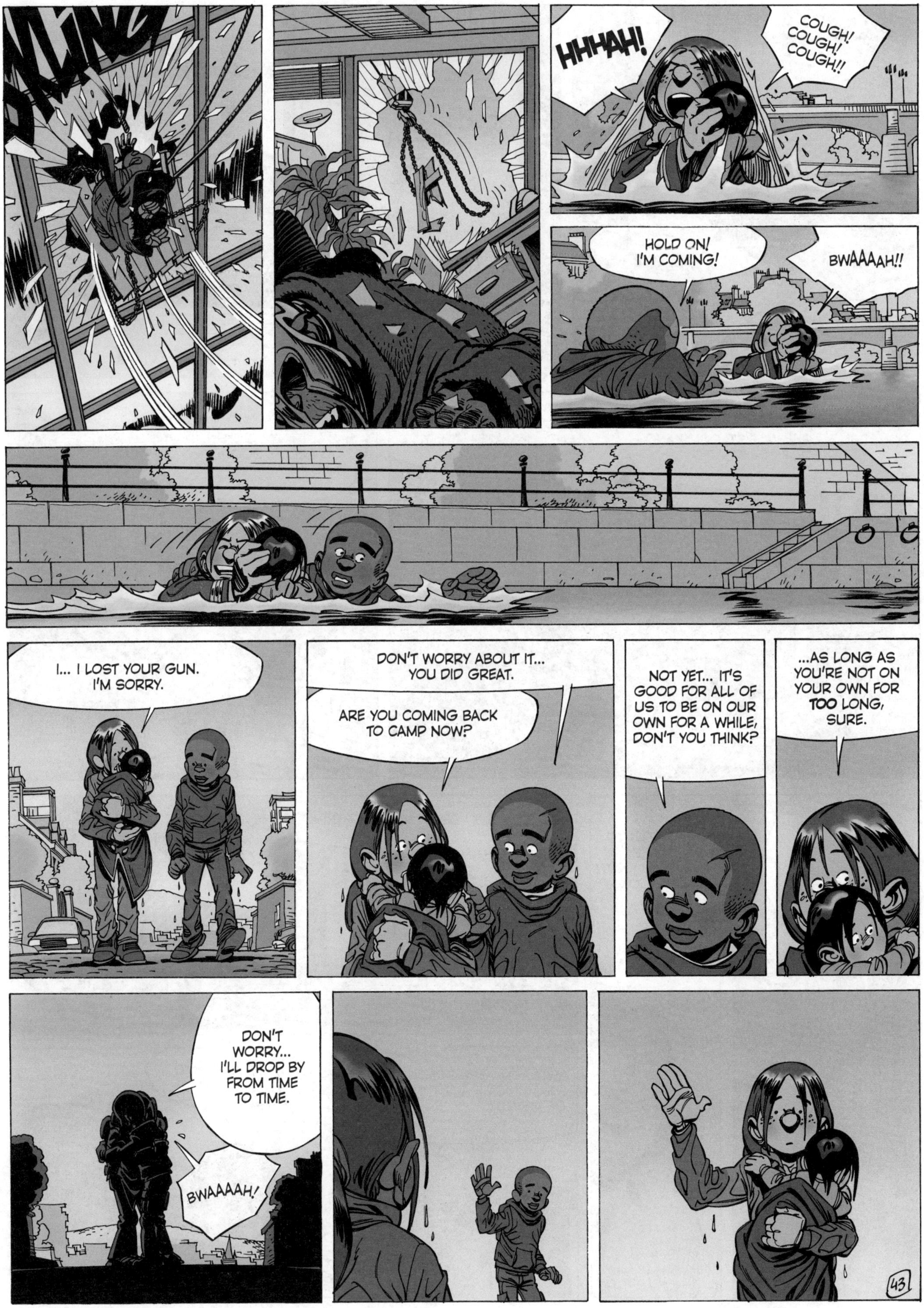
HHHAH!
COUGH! COUGH! COUGH!!
HOLD ON! I'M COMING!
BWAAAAH!!
I... I LOST YOUR GUN. I'M SORRY.
DON'T WORRY ABOUT IT... YOU DID GREAT.
ARE YOU COMING BACK TO CAMP NOW?
NOT YET... IT'S GOOD FOR ALL OF US TO BE ON OUR OWN FOR A WHILE, DON'T YOU THINK?
...AS LONG AS YOU'RE NOT ON YOUR OWN FOR TOO LONG, SURE.
DON'T WORRY... I'LL DROP BY FROM TIME TO TIME.
BWAAAAH!
43

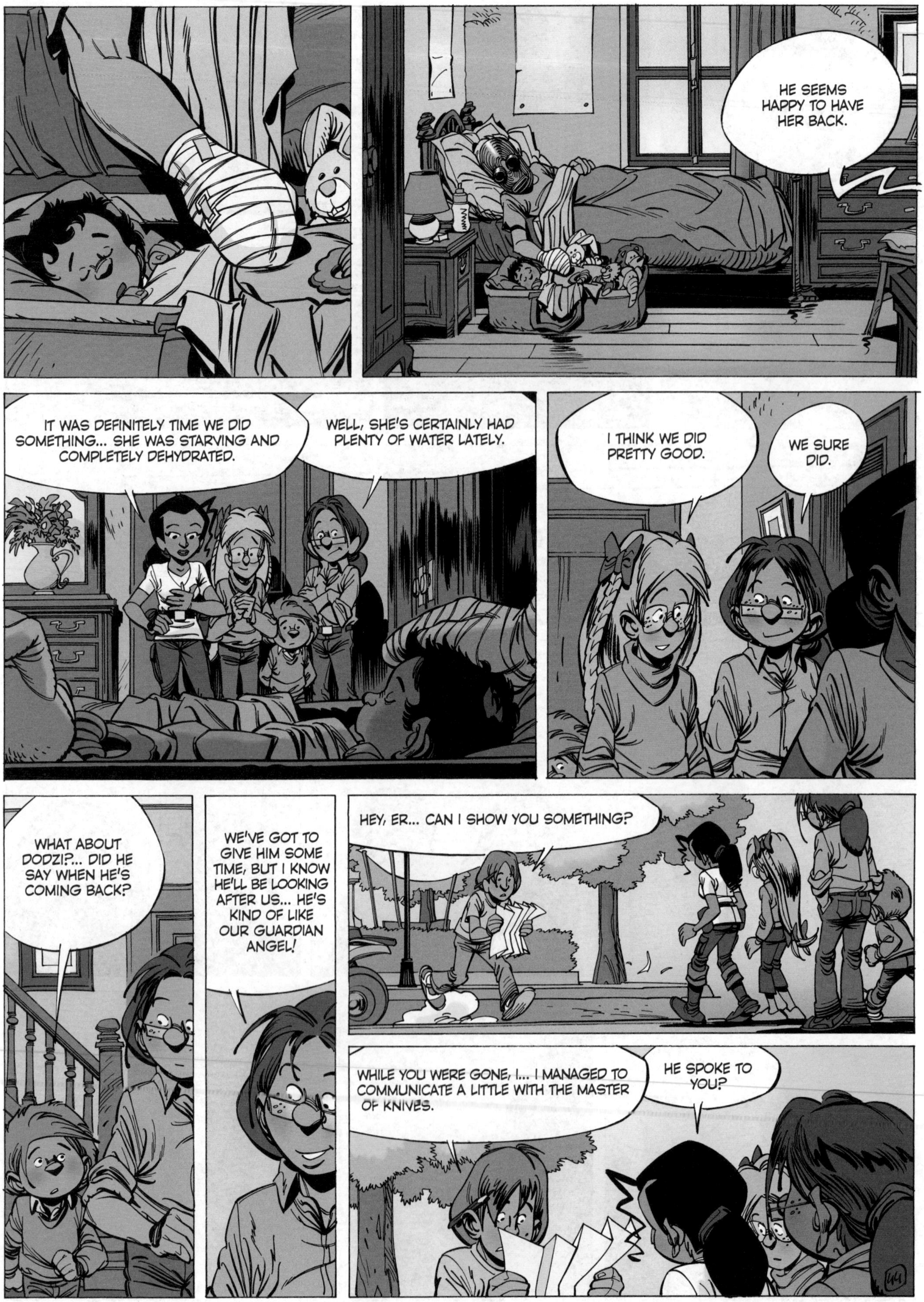
HE SEEMS HAPPY TO HAVE HER BACK.
IT WAS DEFINITELY TIME WE DID SOMETHING... SHE WAS STARVING AND COMPLETELY DEHYDRATED.
WELL, SHE'S CERTAINLY HAD PLENTY OF WATER LATELY.
I THINK WE DID PRETTY GOOD.
WE SURE DID.
WHAT ABOUT DODZI?... DID HE SAY WHEN HE'S COMING BACK?
WE'VE GOT TO GIVE HIM SOME TIME, BUT I KNOW HE'LL BE LOOKING AFTER US... HE'S KIND OF LIKE OUR GUARDIAN ANGEL!
HEY, ER... CAN I SHOW YOU SOMETHING?
WHILE YOU WERE GONE, I... I MANAGED TO COMMUNICATE A LITTLE WITH THE MASTER OF KNIVES.
HE SPOKE TO YOU?

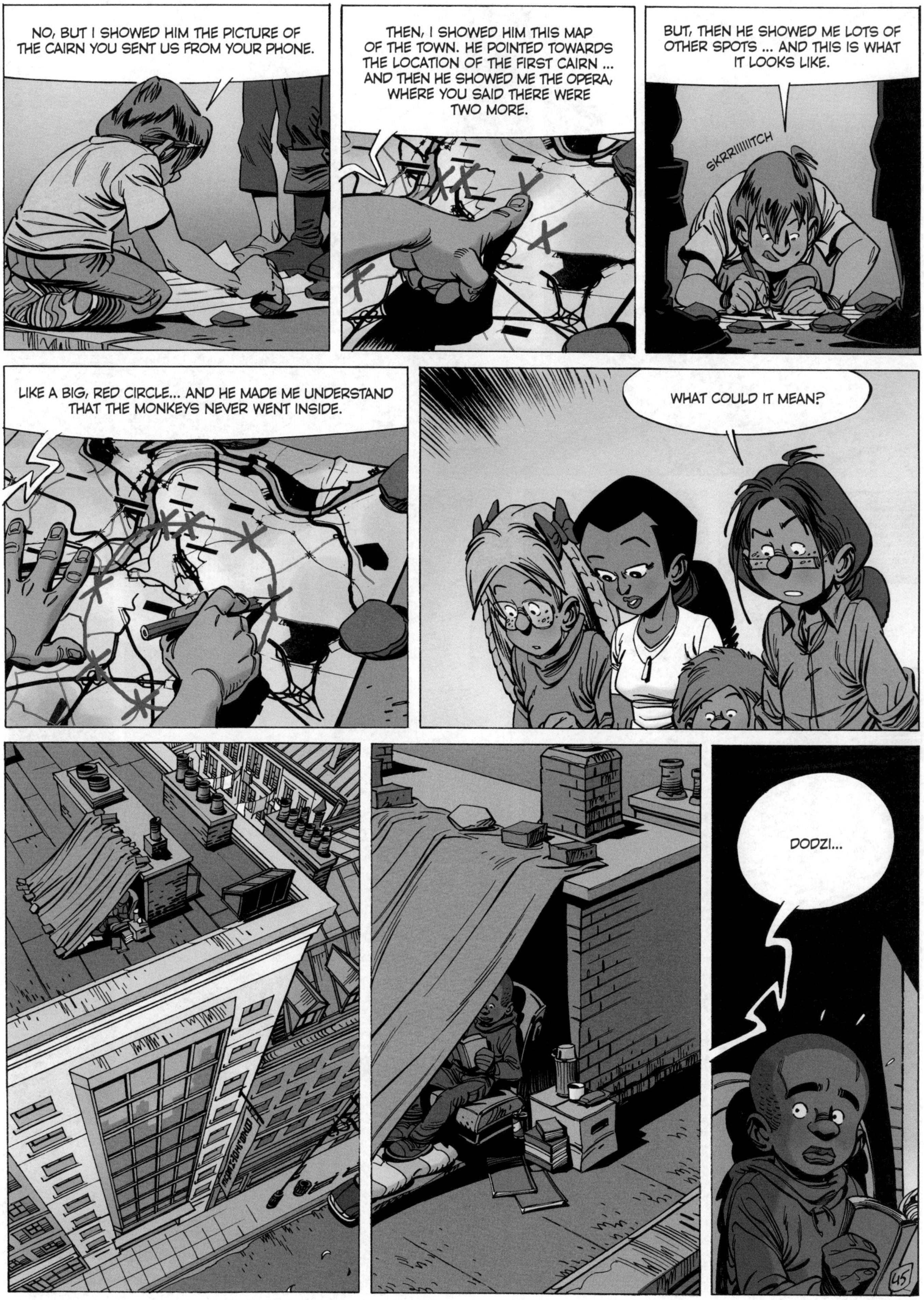

NO, BUT I SHOWED HIM THE PICTURE OF THE CAIRN YOU SENT US FROM YOUR PHONE.
THEN, I SHOWED HIM THIS MAP OF THE TOWN. HE POINTED TOWARDS THE LOCATION OF THE FIRST CAIRN ... AND THEN HE SHOWED ME THE OPERA, WHERE YOU SAID THERE WERE TWO MORE.
BUT, THEN HE SHOWED ME LOTS OF OTHER SPOTS ... AND THIS IS WHAT IT LOOKS LIKE.
SKRRIIIIIIITCH
LIKE A BIG, RED CIRCLE... AND HE MADE ME UNDERSTAND THAT THE MONKEYS NEVER WENT INSIDE.
WHAT COULD IT MEAN?
DODZI...

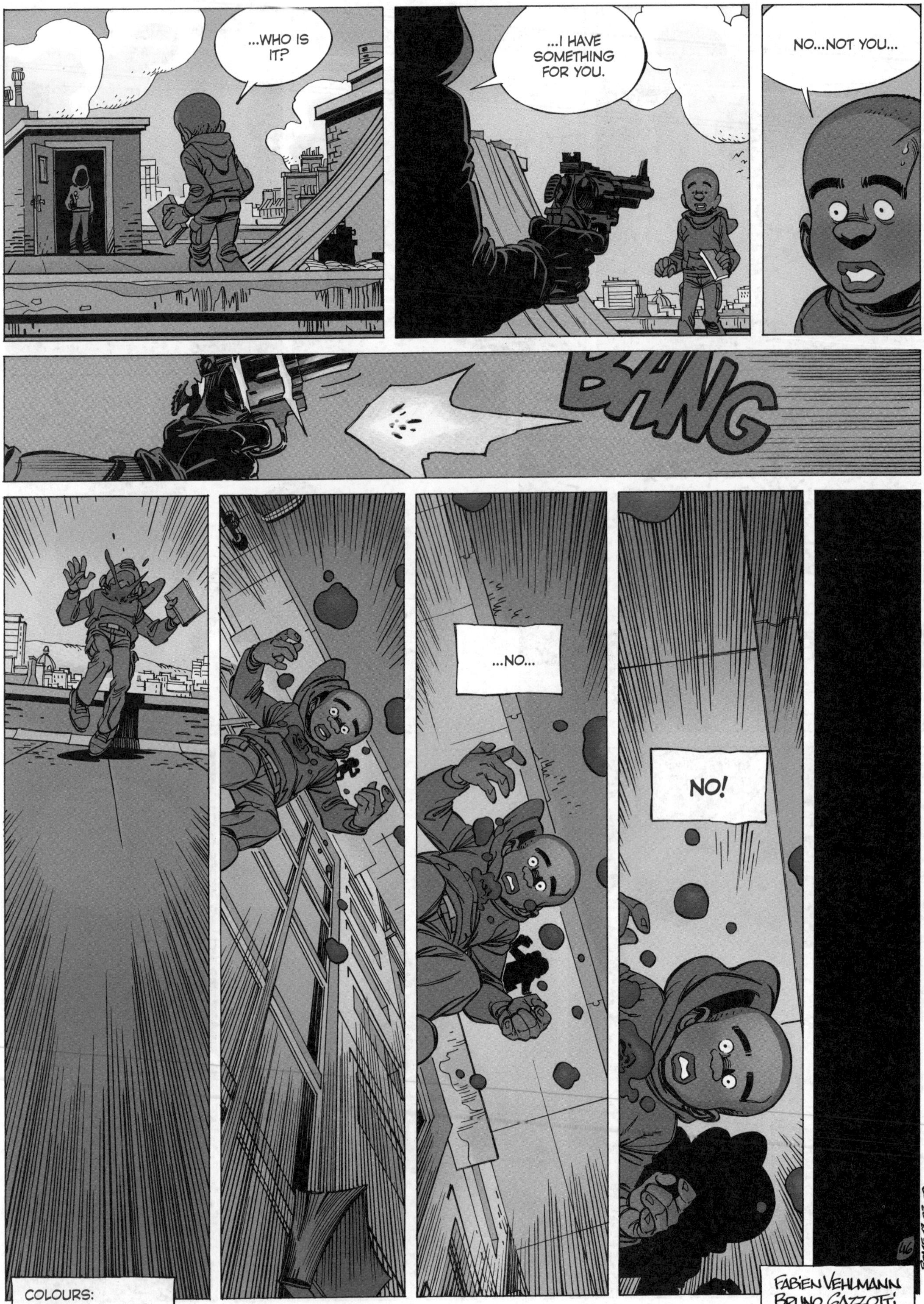
...WHO IS IT?
...I HAVE SOMETHING FOR YOU.
NO...NOT YOU...
BLANG
...NO...
NO!
COLOURS: CAROLINE & USAGI
FABIEN VEHLMANN
BRUNO GAZZOTTI